I Found The Love Of My Life On The Internet!

THERE CAN BE NO DISTANCE BETWEEN TWO LOVING HEARTS!

Edward A. Harris

authorHOUSE®

AuthorHouse™
1663 Liberty Drive
Bloomington, IN 47403
www.authorhouse.com
Phone: 1-800-839-8640

First published by AuthorHouse 10/6/2010

ISBN: 978-1-4520-8637-8 (sc)
ISBN: 978-1-4520-8638-5 (hc)
ISBN: 978-1-4520-8639-2 (e)

Library of Congress Control Number: 2010915029

Printed in the United States of America

This book is printed on acid-free paper.

ACKNOWLEDGEMENTS

I am sincerely grateful to Melody, the Love of My Life, for her taking the journey of our lifetime with me in cyberspace, and to my son – Keith, special friends Priestley, Joycie, Vincent and others who shared my dream as I searched for happiness - which is now reality! God's richest blessings be upon you all!

Special thanks to my Publishing Team for their support in turning my dream of being a published author into reality.

ABOUT THE AUTHOR – EDWARD ALPHONSO HARRIS

Edward Harris is Guyanese by birth, currently a Nationalised Saint Lucian who has travelled extensively and lived in several countries outside of his homeland – Guyana, including Barbados, Dominica, Grenada, Jamaica and Saint Lucia, Sierra Leone and Tanzania.

He is tireless in his quest to share the Principles of Affirmation and to set alight the power of Entrepreneurial Spirit as a means of alleviating poverty around the world.

Edward Harris is a Biblicist, and at 67, he refuses to retire. He is passionate about using the internet to share his life's experiences in the areas of Biblical Principles, Business, Love Relations, Politics and Social Responsibility.

His business and professional experiences are currently applied in the following areas:– Business & Public Relations Consulting, Real Estate Services, Sales & Marketing, Freelance Journalism, Networking, Motivational Speaking and Private Sector & Social Responsibility Advocacy.

http://www.stluciasimplybeautiful.com

FOREWORD

This book is dedicated to those persons everywhere who seek to find true happiness. Especially those who are at the point of giving up but have not tried finding the love of their life on the Internet, or have ventured into cyberspace but are frustrated due to the abuse by persons with whom they sought to establish genuine relationships. I implore you to take a last stand – try a reputable on line relationship service!

It is my hope that you will get the confidence to go forward, believing that it is possible to find loving and respectful individuals in our world today, even on the Internet. I did not only find the Love of my life on the Internet – I found a Family on the Internet. It is for this reason that Melody and I have agreed to share our story with the world. There are lessons to be learnt from our experiences and the task has been ours to share - We Love You!

CONTENTS

CHAPTER ONE –
LOVE DEFIES DISTANCE - THE INITIAL JOURNEY!!!

Our Creator always grants us the desires of our hearts whether it is for better or for worse. That is the power of choice - to choose good or evil! I began my search for a partner who will meet my expectations and be my help meet seven years ago, in between there were relationships but the search continued, until on the morning of the 8th of June 2010, in the height of my frustration, I sat in front of my desk top computer and headed for MSN Search to find a Pen Pal Group. I came upon a listing that attracted me and with a click I was introduced to http://www.12meetsenior.com (in spite of the name, it is a site for all ages).

I reviewed the home page and took advantage of viewing the other pages available to visitors which gave me confidence to proceed with registering as a free member. By day two I decided to become a paid subscriber. The first fan I selected was Melody who was born in Zimbabwe but is currently resident in Tanzania. I sent off the usual introductory email to her but it dawned on me that it was a great distance between us and major differences in cultures. However, I persisted having assured myself that no distance should prevent two people of like minds from sharing each other's life.

I never thought in my wildest dreams that a relationship on the internet could have been so intense. In the short time of fifty nine (59) days, a journey which commenced on the 8th June, 2010, finally culminated on the morning of the 6th of August, 2010 when I was warmly greeted at Julius Nyerere International Airport, Tanzania, embraced and welcomed by Melody! It was a moment in time that I will always remember.

We planned to spend three days in Dar es Salaam upon Melody's insistence that she will meet me on my arrival on Tanzanian soil and show me around the Capital, but we only spent a day and a night before we headed for my final destination – Arusha. It was a quiet Saturday afternoon as we drove to my new home which I share with Melody who is a widow and two of her five children, ages 25 and 2. The others are at Universities in England and South Africa.

I must admit I was unaware of the environment I was entering as Melody never sent photographs of her home and surroundings. She kept that as a surprise in spite we exchanged a lot of photographs. I trusted her judgment and within the short space of time in which we communicated via the internet, she gained my confidence.

As I discussed my impending departure from my home in Saint Lucia for more than 30 years and leaving behind established relations in business and with many friends, the question which was being asked all the time was – are you sure you are going to be OK with all the negative stories we hear happening in Africa? I repeated again and again that "I trust Melody". In the latter stages, we talked daily on the phone, sometimes I gave my friends the opportunity to speak with her so at least they will know she is real.

Like Melody, I have five children and my eldest son was relieved of his own concerns when I arranged for us to meet on SKYPE and the two sides met – Melody and her daughters, and my son – Keith and I. It was a bit difficult to establish the internet connection but we did finally. The photographs and persons we spoke with matched. At least I cleared a major hurdle in relation to my going to a country in the middle of Africa without knowing who I was going to. Photographs were not enough, it needed more and from that moment my son was fully on my side.

Tanzania is ahead of US EST by seven hours during Summer. During the period of our relationship, we spoke on the telephone, and we communicated by email, a minimum of twice daily. We woke up to a love note in the morning and went to bed after reading another at night. In between, during our waking hours as the feelings allowed, shorter notes and other bits of information were exchanged. Three hundred and thirty three (333) emails were exchanged in just under two (2) months prior to our meeting in person.

This is how it started:

2010-06-08 07:50:59

Hello Stranger,

Thanks for making me one of your favourites.

I like your profile and your pictures are just stunning.

So, do you care to communicate with me?

If you like, then we can.

I will be waiting for your response.

Be blessed

Melody

2010-06-08 19:12:25

Dear Melody,

Great to have you as a friend. Thank you for your observations about my profile and pictures.

I will hope that you can tell more about your country.

I have a few of my own websites which I will introduce to you so you can get a glimpse of my busy lifestyle.

Ed.

COMMENT:

Welcome to the world of Melody and Ed, enjoy the ride!

CHAPTER TWO –
THREE MIRACLE WORDS – I LOVE YOU!!!

If there is one lesson I have learnt from our relationship is that truth which is found in the Holy Scriptures. LOVE is the greatest commandment. In my communication with Melody, I discovered three words that should be the theme of every relationship – I LOVE YOU! We began to use those three words freely and they became a unifying force between us, it bonded us together. I Love You!

When I use the miracle words, it causes me to pause and reflect upon my deep devotion to Melody and the respect I have for her. As our relationship grew, those three words gave us strength to move the process of our coming together even at a faster pace. I felt like I had known Melody for several years and I got the feeling that both of us felt this way.

As we progress along life's path together, we will keep true to our commitment of repeating the miracle words as if it is a mantra, regardless of the place and time, even in the middle of the night, we will exchange those miracle words – I Love You! Sometimes we communicate in whispers, and sometimes audibly. There is magic in those words, we have committed to using the three miracle words as often as the opportunity presents itself. Love removes all conflicts; Love finds a way not only sometimes, but every time.

COMMENT
We discovered three simple words with very powerful impact – I Love You!

CHAPTER THREE –
BE SINCERE – GENUINE RELATIONSHIPS ARE BUILT ON TRUST!!!

The title of this chapter is so fundamental that if applied in any relationship can only have life changing effects for the better in every aspect of our lives. I am obliged always to seek clear definition of such fundamental words as SINCERE! The dictionary at my disposal (Oxford English Reference) reveals the meaning of Sincere to be: 1. Free from pretence or deceit: the same in reality as in appearance. 2. Genuine, honest, frank.

The relationship which Melody and I have established and currently share would not have been possible without trust and sincerity of purpose. On both sides, there were lots at stake, family being the most important. As mature individuals, we had to take each step responsibly and seek to get our children on our sides. We were fortunate, that this was the easy part. We trusted our Creator in many ways to see us through. He truly gives us the desires of our hearts. We prayed for and affirmed the victory that is ours today.

Every step of the way, we opened up to each other and shared without holding back anything to the point it could be said figuratively that we declared our opening balance sheets. We knew everything we needed to know about each other that set the platform that we will build our present and future relationship upon.

The letters we exchanged were so reassuring that confidence naturally emerged on both sides. I was confident in leaving behind family, friends, social and business relationships that I built up over a period of thirty years, and she was prepared to open her heart, her family and her home to me.

COMMENT:
The stage has been set for a solid foundation that will be strong in spite of whatever challenges, as always in the process of really getting to know each other, there must be concessions on both sides but the mantra – "I Love You" is sure to give us the power to triumph over any obstacle.

CHAPTER FOUR –
DON'T ONLY SAY IT – WRITE IT!!!

Don't only say it, write it. Any motivational speaker of note always exhorts his/her audience to write down whatever their goals are and commit them to memory. Then, Self Talk your written ideas and goals into reality. The objective is for you to live your dreams even before they become reality. Open up your attractive force, so that you will be seen as you expect to be seen. You will wake up to the reality that the forces necessary to take you to your destination begin to turn up and align themselves with your cause.

Melody and I have written our way to each other's heart with an indelible ink where the words of love that we exchanged are now in control of our lives, we live our words. The letters we exchanged made it happen for us. Words have very powerful effect on the recipient. "The pen is mightier than the sword" Words when used effectively cut through to the heart with laser like precision. We mutually agreed on this point. The truth is that Melody really has her way with words as you will soon experience but in every instance her words are seasoned with sincerity.

COMMENT:
As a result of the transformation which has taken place in our lives, we have decided to write a series of e-books, including our autobiographies in an effort to share our experiences on many subjects that will touch hearts and change lives around the world.

CHAPTER FIVE –
SELECTED EMAILS EXCHANGED!!!

We have come to the part that this book is all about. We have carefully selected eighty six (86) emails to show a clear path as to how our relationship progressed up to the moment when I boarded the flight on British Airways from London to Dar es Salaam, Tanzania on the 5th of August, 2010.

The trip was very enjoyable, no moment of anxiety as a result of turbulence, except for the anticipation of my meeting with Melody. I kept relying on Melody's favorite words in moments of uncertainty as we planned my trip to Tanzania – "Everything will be fine!" I will be first to say she has delivered. Everything has been fine ever since my arrival!

We invite you to share in our fairy tale kind of relationship where the written word has taken us up to the mountain top of reality. It is our sincere wish that our readers will benefit from the approach we applied to bring us to together in almost a magical way.

#1 Melody introduces herself and family
June 9, 2010
Dear Ed,

Hello once more, or should I say good afternoon Ed. Its 4:30pm here and there I gather its 9:30 am, so we are 7 hours ahead of you.

We are about to go home, in one hour's time, while you will be starting your day. Oh, so you have a hectic schedule? We say Pole sana in Kiswahili, meaning something like sorry for that or I sympathise with you. Maybe, I should actually say, just enjoy your day in spite of it all. Funny!

I was trying to visualize all the globetrotting that you have done so far and are about to do. That's really something. You know what, you amaze me. So you have been to Sierra Leone? You mean you stood where the Africans were being shipped away as slaves? Oh God, Edward, even if I might not have been there, but I can still feel the pain for them. Even some of us whose ancestors remained here in Africa, they underwent some form of slavery under the colonial regimes. It was just terrible, evil and outrageous. God have mercy!

Let me put my office in order and go home. I will continue with this email home after I would have rested a bit.

I am home now and my time is 9:15pm

Since I said I will send you my family's picture, here it is.

You want to know the number of children I have - I suppose? Well l have sent you a family picture that was taken 5 months ago when all the children were home on holidays. I have a large family. To be exact, I have five children, four daughters and a son. Except for my two year old daughter, my children are all adults, unmarried, and in the final stages of their professional qualifications. I even adopted a daughter who is not in the family photo. She followed in my footsteps and got married rather early. Here is a picture of my adopted daughter with me and her baby I am holding.

Please don't run away from our friendship due to fear of my big family. They are well cultured children and we are a close knit family. They will adore you, if they get to know you. The thing they are after is my happiness. We are very open with each other. Maybe it's due to the fact that they have been living away from home most of the time. Also these kids have been trained to apply themselves. Most credit goes to God on high who gave them the brains. Otherwise, it could not have been possible.

My little baby was not planned at all. It was just an accidental blessing. Even with my other children, I did not plan at all, as a result the spacing was poorly done as you can see that there was no time / space between each of them, almost every year a baby kind of thing.

You can see how traditional and unsophisticated I have been in not practicing family planning in earnest, or should I say, I am a woman with a high fertility genetic makeup? I just don't know.

I also started early. Since I had married my secondary school teacher, all my tertiary education was done whilst playing the role of wife, mother and student at the same time. I just thank God for giving me the brains and the capability.

My dear Edward, so you can see my family and now you know more about me, isn't it? You are free to ask me anything, I mean anything about me and my family even about my late husband. Feel free about that. If somehow you don't want to hear about that part of my life, please let me know so that I won't annoy you with reference to that- right?

What I know is that they will like you very much, when they get to know about you. At the moment, they know that we are friends and they are fine with that.

So how many children do you have? Do you mind me asking about your family - your wife, etc.? Please let me know if you are not comfortable with my questions. I will respect your feelings. Also, if you somehow feel that my family is too big and you don't like a friend with all these children, I will still respect your feelings. So feel free to express your true feelings. You can even joke about my family, everyone will take it; we are such a merry bunch.

So Ed, tell me, what do you say about me now?

What else will you want to know? I am a person who just expresses what I feel at any moment. Do you have any problems with that dear?

Sorry for this abnormally long letter. In my future emails, I will try to summarize the topic.

I am eagerly awaiting your reply.

Take care,

Melody

COMMENT: In the past I did my best to avoid relationships where children were involved but I willingly pursued this relationship putting all my fears behind me to be a part of the family with a promise to love my adopted two year old and be a Father to her which I never was to my five children.

#2 Edward replies to Melody's introductory letter

June 9, 2010

Dear Melody,

I read your letter twice, checked the pictures and verified everyone. Don't forget, I am a freelance journalist, so you can write as long emails as you like. I will surely read them. I like reading, just as much as I like writing.

You are a great woman. God has been good to you and your family. You will be OK very soon and your last baby will be the cherished daughter of all your children. I hope your adopted daughter will emulate you and not be put off by the set back with her lack of education due to early marriage. I was also married at 19 the first time. I have been married more times that I care to remember. Unfortunately for me, I was married four times. My last wedding was held in Bronx, New York, 150 guests, restaurant on the sea, shrimp dinner. There was a skit and a floor show at the wedding, 5 stretch limos, etc. The marriage only survived 5 years. We are still friends and we talk regularly. There is one thing that I feel blessed about is that I continue to maintain a cordial relationship with all my wives, two of whom had no offspring.

I am very unsettled at the moment. I am very uneasy about my life, but somehow happy. I have great friends who look out for me and we spend a lot of time together. I have five children all adults, 3 in New York - 2 boys and 1 girl, a girl in Guyana and a boy in St. Lucia. Their ages range from 37 - 25. They are all doing well except for my eldest child who is now getting into her own, and blessed me with twin grandsons.

I have done nothing much today. Just got up and have to write my article. Hope the moments spent writing to you will inspire me to write my best article yet.

Please send me some details about your adopted country. A website link could help.

Yours,

Ed.

Comment:

Melody was ahead of the game as she knew a lot about Ed in the History provided on the website and the accompanying ten photographs allowed on the site. Please feel free to check out my profile on the site referred to earlier.

#3 Melody gets closer to a Commitment

June 10, 2010

Heya,

I have fallen in love with your picture you sent. It's so real, like you looking at me. You are so adorable. Oh God, I hope you understand me.

At long last I managed to create a Gmail account especially for you. You will never know how I am starting to feel for you. You are so different. I just like a lot about you. You are just so unbelievable. What am I supposed to say? How can I tell you exactly how I feel without losing my womanly pride? Oh Ed, I even like your name so much. I love the way you write to me. You are just too good to be true.

Yes, I am still awake. I have been reading all your mails again and again to try to understand every bit of everything about you. You are my mystery. I have gone through your websites to try and see what you do and what makes you tick. Ed, I am impressed, that is all I can say.

Yes, it's late now, I know but reading all about you is worth it all. Even if you get angry with me for not responding to your mail promptly, it's still worth it.

I love your article, have even printed it. I am tempted even to frame it. I will write about it tomorrow. You are a great writer, are you aware of that? You are such a genius and a very lovable person. About the request, consider it granted - LOL. I will/can do whatever you want me to do, any time. Should I say your wish is my command Ed? What are friends there for? I am starting to feel you in my life.

Enjoy your nap. I am starting to feel like a very close friend of mine Ed.

Melody

#4 Melody follows up

Heya,

Actually you were on my mind constantly. Are you not surprised that I am missing you way too much for someone whom I am just getting to know? I am wondering how is this possible?

Well tell me, how has been your day so far? Thanks for the Newsletter, I will read it. By the way tomorrow I will give you a feed back on your wonderful article.

It's night time here now. Want to know something, I am feeling lonelier than ever before? I feel a void somehow - somewhere. Well, I just don't know what it is all about. I also find myself looking at your pictures all the time. It makes me feel like I will get to know you better just by looking at it. It seems like your picture communicates with my inner being. It looks like it gives me inspiration, reason to carry on, to look forward to tomorrow. Ever heard of such insanity Ed?

Thank you for the phone call. Thanks for your concern. You make a difference in my life. Your voice is very comforting. You made me feel good. I just wished if you had been here in person. I got so excited talking to you, so much that I wonder whether I was making sense at all. It's just unbelievable.

Don't feel blue at all my dear Ed. I am here for you. I will try to be available for you. You said you wished if you were still young? Let me tell you something, I just like you the way you are. You are the perfect age for me, for our friendship. I adore your wisdom and maturity.

About the picture, I look really big in that picture isn't it? You know what - just to have someone who comments on such things as pictures and so on is a blessing. I am getting to realize that now. With no one to see, comment, or even complain about something or anything is so lonely.

I am just discovering the loneliness of not having someone to share my life with. It's just terrible. It's just terrible to be alone. Well, one might have loving children who have one's best interest at heart, but still the fact remains, it's still lonely somehow. It is the type of loneliness that is hard to define, that is not so obvious but is only felt. The hidden void, it's a loneliness that is only perceived by the heart, not the eyes. Oh Ed, let me stop this – right? At least I have you as a friend, it's no longer that lonely I suppose. You are just filling a void in my life somehow in your own special way, though far away but somehow you are a part of my life. A good friend, I believe I can trust. That is who I would want you to be. You seem so sweet, loving and considerate Ed. I can still hear your voice in my ear and it's such a lullaby.

I would also want you to enjoy your day. I wish you all the best things you yearn for in life. Please, always remember that you can count on me anytime. I will always be here for you whenever you might need me.

Melody

#5 Ed acknowledges Melody's comforting words

June 12, 2010

Hello Melody,

It is after midnight. I just got home but couldn't go to bed without checking my mail to see if you sent an email for me and you did! I am so comforted by your warm and considerate words. Why is there so much distance between us? I feel I can fly to meet you right at this moment. I have never communicated with someone who expresses herself/himself as you do. I am ecstatic!

This is getting out of hand. I can't help myself. I am first to admit words are powerful and you do make something happen inside of me. You are so spirited. I like the energy between us. I woke up at 6.00 am and it is now after midnight and I still have energy to write to you after a marvelous evening.

I am listening to some great music on the radio. Life is so wonderful; I visited the Calypso Tent early this afternoon, took my friend home, and spent some time with him at his home, about 2 hours before going to another engagement.

Good morning and look forward to hearing from you as the day progresses. Maybe, I will await your reply before I go to sleep.

Regards,

Ed

#6 Ed & Melody begin to look at travel options

June 13, 2010

Hello Ed,

I will find out for you, the best way to travel to my country by tomorrow morning. I am so excited to say the least.

Oh Ed we just had a power cut, its common here and my lap top only has 10% of power left, had not charged it. I will phone though.

Ed you have been everywhere so it seems. If it's not asking a lot from you could you consider coming over here first my love? That would be like heaven to me. Then afterwards we could plan going wherever you want to take me with you. What do you think?

Tomorrow, I will just inquire from a travel office in our building complex about travelling from St. Lucia to Arusha, Tanzania - right? I will send you all the details.

I could give anything Ed, for me to have you here even just for one weekend if you don't have enough time. Yes, I can give anything just to be with you. Just to be close to you. I am dying to see you my love.

Let me send this before this laptop goes out of power. I am prepared to give you my all.

Melody

#7 Ed shares with Melody his spiritual and professional values, including his Curriculum Vitae

June 13, 2010

Dearest Melody,

I spent most of my afternoon/evening thinking about you and writing to you. Since you said that Sunday is your rest day I don't feel comfortable overloading you with homework. However, I thought I send you my CV which is abridged; the unabridged version was several pages more. I thought of sending you a Sunday Laugh as I know at the end of my resume' you will wonder how could such an uneducated boy achieve so much. That is the miracle power of AFFIRMATION and as Napoleon Hill in his book Think and Grow Rich fitly made the point "Whatever the mind can conceive and believe, it can achieve." The Founders of the "SECRET" taught us to BELIEVE, ASK, RECEIVE! You can check this out on their site and view their documentary THE SECRET www.thesecret.tv You can get a free copy of Think and Grow Rich on line just do a search for the book, I read the book 3 times. Tonight you have been empowered even when you are asleep. Maybe, you had your first dream about us.

God is great! I believe in Miracles, you are my latest miracle. I can't begin to imagine how in one week so much has happened and here we are, - loving it! What a Mighty God we serve? Pray for me and remember in everything give thanks because it is the will of Christ Jesus concerning us. I hope that you will awake with a fulfilled expectation - a mouthful from me.

Have a blessed Sunday,

Ed

#8 Ed and Melody begin to think seriously about their coming together

June 20, 2010

Dear Melody,

Hope your night was great and you arose in a spirit of giving God thanks for the week past and ask his blessings for the ensuing week. God is great! We have come this far and now await the countdown to my getting to Arusha. I have counted 19 weeks as of Monday 21st June, 2010, four and a half months to go. That is like eternity.

Whatever you do, whether you go to church or not, please pray for me. The power of writing it down is real. Just talking about October, it seems near but when it is written down there are a lot of months ahead not to mention weeks. Well the longest road has an end and our waiting will one day soon be over.

The weather is not good over the past few days. It has been raining a lot. There is a prediction for a busy hurricane season. Last year was great, very little activity but not so this time, the indications are very much here.

Well, I guess you are having a busy time catching up on your reading the e-books I sent you. Please take your time. I guess you are already losing weight with the intense pressure of writing and reading. It may be a tall order. Do you want us to take a rest in the new week, no telephone calls, and no emails, how does that sound. It seems impossible to me as if I don't hear from you in a few hours I have to call you; how could I be silent for a week? Doesn't look feasible but maybe you will like to test your will power. What sayest thou? Sometimes, I feel I wear you down with my pace. Do you need my sympathy? I feel in my heart that you are capable so I will intensify the demands next week rather than give you a break.

Did I promise not to lead? I promised to be faithful to my darling and let her be the leader. I drove you real hard in our first few days. This is tremendous, the intensity is so strong. What will it be when we meet?

I feel our meeting should be video recorded. Those will be moments to be cherished. Maybe, I will be able to pick up a Camcorder on my trip to China. Are you excited about our coming together - even now?

No lesson tonight. I will be kind. I will do some home work on my own. Study Arusha, read up on CIA Fact Sheet, etc. I will do some serious research on Tanzania so as to identify a niche. How many newspapers are there in Tanzania or more specifically in Arusha? I have several articles I can reproduce from my archive. Writing a weekend column could be an effortless reality. So can we put that on the list of possible projects for your consideration and approval? That could be a natural path to my motivational speaking and business training programmes.

Darling I miss you, I need you, I love you!!!!!!!!

Love Always,

Ed

#9 Melody responds

June 22, 2010

Hello Ed,

You should be still asleep. My sleep was good but short. I slept late.

I will pray for you, as I always do.

You talked of waiting, it's not easy, but definitely we will be getting together in October – that's soon. Time has a way of passing swiftly.

That weather should calm down. We should pray that there be no hurricane. That weather should improve. You are needed here well, alive and kicking.

Today I looked at your Facebook profile. I like your picture.

You talked of giving me a break? You made me laugh. Do you see that possible my love? That would make me develop hypertension or stress. I think the stage we have reached is too far gone to hold back the momentum that our relationship has achieved to date. Can I manage living without your mail or/and telephone calls? I would lose it I suppose. I can't even imagine how it would feel like.

Darling you are a born leader - that goes without saying. I will then be your manager my love. Just being next to you is enough for me.

Whenever I hear Beyonce Knowle's song "HALO" It just reminds me of our relationship. I am crazy for your love Ed my darling. I CAN FEEL YOUR LOVE within my heart.

I AM MORE THAN LOOKING FORWARD to your coming and it seems I can't wait. Being excited is an understatement.

On the issue of writing a weekend column in the Arusha papers I will enquire into that. I will keep you updated on any information I get. It should be very possible. Yes, we must put it on the list of possible projects.

Our meeting should be memorable. It should be the most important event in our life. Indeed you are the most important thing that ever happened to me, indeed time will stand still.

Sweetheart, I am living this life for you. You are the reason for many things in my life now. I think I love and need you more than ever before.

Good morning my love. Enjoy your new day. Ed, you mean the world to me.

Melody

#10 Melody expresses feelings of loneliness
June 22, 2010
Darling Ed,

Good Evening!

It should be afternoon there. I miss you terribly; the nights are lonelier now somehow. Some days are diamond, some days are stone. Well let's just keep on expecting the best. The best way is just to try to take everything easy.

I love you Ed. Everything is going to work out in our best interest, that I know. I have attached the song. Well I assume it should be the one. I have fallen in love with it. So enjoy it with me – Anne Murray – Can I have this dance!

You made me laugh by saying your dog is a priest. I just think he is selective. Maybe he did not fall in love with that particular bitch. It's funny, isn't it? So when you come here, where will you leave the dog? What's his name? I grew up with dogs. I even had my own puppy at some point. Otherwise, how are you? How did it go at the vet?

The thing that's making me go on is the fact that, no matter what, you will be coming. I miss you my darling. The nights are worse. I just wish to be close to you. I miss your company. I feel so lonely even if there is company. What I am longing for - is you! Only you my love!

I will sleep a bit late. You should try to rest/relax a bit. Ed my love, you are constantly on my mind. I am counting the days and it seems to be very long to October. Still it's better to have something to look forward to, no matter how long it seems to be taking. I will wait for you darling, no matter how long it might seem to be taking. You are my everything!

I really love you my dear man. Well my love, enjoy the remainder of the day. Never forget that you mean the world to me.

Melody

#11 Ed Commits
June 23, 2010
Dear Melody,

Good morning Melody!

It must be a beautiful morning. Hope you had a great night. My night so far has been hectic, fighting with the computer and have to get back here early to prepare for the presentation I have to make. Never in my public life have I had to present someone else's work but I was given the liberty to add my two cents.

Darling, in spite of my hectic lifestyle, I still have time to think of you. I didn't get to listen to the song. I was working on costing the inventory for a property I sold, among other things. I love you baby and working as hard as I can to realize the necessary financial requirement to make it happen. I am starting from zero. It has been a long struggle, although I made money in recent times and will continue to do so as long as there is life. But you know what, because of the scale and scope of things here I feel I have to put out too much for too little. I am ready to start a new life in a new environment with the love of my life - Melody!

I try not to think about it, but I have to agree with my friends who over the years encouraged me to migrate to one of the developed countries as they felt the Caribbean was too slow for me. It is not too late to move to a place with more possibilities. I have a good life here but I need to get a bit more out of life. I am depending on us to make it happen. I will work as hard as it takes to achieve the best for us. When

I think about the situation, sometimes I feel helpless. I am never one to give up. I am a perpetual optimist. Darling you are my future, I love you without seeing you in person, and you have transmitted your warm affections to me. I can't help myself. I keep falling in love with you more and more with every passing moment.

My friend came to visit me tonight and we were talking briefly about the future. I showed him your unclassified pictures on the net. He has approved of you and is supportive of me and our future plans. He is a very special friend, we communicate with each other every day when we are on island and socialize a lot. He visits my home all the time and will visit us in due course.

Well be good, I feel that the hassle in my life is over and you will be right by my side to embrace the future. We are going to be a great couple. I must go now but you are on my mind. As always, I love you endlessly!

Ed

#12 Melody commits

June 23, 2010

Edward my love,

Good Afternoon!

It has been a good day so far. I am busy but my day is not as hectic as yours my love. It is a beautiful day. The good thing about this place is the beautiful weather. We are supposed to be near the Equator but still it is warm to cool in Arusha, a great contrast to the other town near the coast, Dar es Salaam, which is humid and very hot.

You just make me laugh. You ask if I would employ you in the event you made a sale. That's so funny. You are already employed. Whether you make a sale or no sale, you are in, LOL. You just blow me away Ed. We are employed by each other, if there is such a thing at all.

So tell me, do you still want to migrate my love? Thank you for thinking of me in all this. I really appreciate your kind thoughts. Ed, you are just amazing.

Let's hope you will manage all what's ahead of you today, for it seems you did not sleep well my love. It just sounds like you have been too busy. I presume once the deals have been concluded you will have time to rest awhile.

23

I have been thinking of you more than you can imagine possible. God bless your friend who is supportive of our love. It's not possible to imagine that a love such as ours is possible. Have I told you lately that I am more than ready to start a new life with you anywhere in the world, even in the desert my love? If you feel Arusha is not ideal, we will wait until the end of the completion of the project I am engaged in and then we can see where to move to. If you fall in love with this part of the world - OK. Even if you opt for Zimbabwe, Harare is great! It would even be better. America, Africa, Australia, the Caribbean or elsewhere, I don't mind as long as I will be with you. You are my reason to go on. You are my happiness. Actually, you are my everything! I keep falling more in love with you. Oh, yes I am.

Ed, you are the only man in my life. I could even write a song. Anyway, my heart is singing for you all day long. I love you, my love. I need you my darling.

The world economy might be bad at the moment but I still believe that you and I can make it against all odds. I am also a self styled optimist. All what I am planning now hinges on our staying together. I am trying to save all the money I can for our life together, after seeing to the comfort of my children.

At least most of my children are grown and will be on their own soon. You and I, we can start afresh and build a future of our own. I thank God that you will be coming whereby we would sit down and plan. Very soon you will know me through and through. No matter what Ed, I will never let you down. I will always love you. I will take care of you. You will be my friend, my lover, my confidante, my closest relative, and most of all my brain, and my husband. Yes you will be part of me. You are already my everything Ed. I trust you and I trust my heart. According to my heart you are the one for me.

When you come here you will find a part of a manuscript of my own writing, a piece of my life. I know with you we can move mountains. Yes we can swim the seas and even reach the moon.

I am continuously falling in love with you Ed, because you understand me. It looks like you even know how I tick inside. You have won my heart dear man. You seem to have known me since time immemorial. Yes Ed, you are the love of my life. I love a lot about you. I Love You!

We will build our future on each other. Trust me my love, you mean all that's worthy to me. You are my destiny Ed. Enjoy the remainder of the day and be further blessed.

You are and you will be the love of my life forever more,
Melody

#13 The role of the Internet

June 23, 2010
HELLO DARLING,

It's always so nice talking with you on the telephone. When you were phoning, I was busy reading your presentation that you want to be put on power point slides. It's so well done, even not yet finished as you say. Want my honest opinion Ed? I admire your being genuine and your originality.

YOU ARE SO GOOD AND PASSIONATE ABOUT WHAT YOU DO AND YOU BELIEVE IN YOURSELF. YOU ARE SO CONVINCING IN WHATEVER YOU SAY. I LOVE SUCH ATTRIBUTES IN A PERSON ESPECIALLY SOMEONE AS CLOSE TO ME AS YOU ARE.

Just judging you by how you write, if I had not known you, I could just as well have been your best fan. If we had grown up together I could have been your best friend. When trying to find a partner, I could still have fought the girls in the world so as to be the love of your life. Lastly, I could have fought all odds to be your life's companion; actually I could even have married you so many times over, if there would have been such a chance.

It sounds funny, isn't it? You really would just as well have won me through the pen. Your pen is indeed mightier than the sword. I love your ethics my dear Edward. I love your style. You are so charming in a very unique way. Please don't take advantage of me since you have won me in every respect. I am already addicted to you my love. I am in a condition of total surrender. You just represent my idea of the ideal masculinity in a man. I can give a lot so as to be your ideal woman. I can even go changing if it calls for that. I would want to answer to all the femininity you may imagine and yearn for in the woman specie.

Oh, by the way I love your pictures. Have I told you lately how I love the way you are? I have been asking myself all along whether this wide world had you in it? Why has it taken so long for us to find each other? I like the internet Edward, for it has defied the many miles between us, and just placed us in the global village in which communicating is done so easily and so quickly as if we are just neighbours. I like the way technology is bring the peoples of the world together.

It just goes without saying that I BELIEVE IN YOU AND ALL WHAT YOU DO, OR ATTEMPT TO DO. I just want you to know that you have the attributes I have been looking for in a man all along, but failing to find until now. You have those rare qualities dear Edward.

I pray that you will not manipulate me because I have just succumbed to your charm and I admire and trust you entirely. I could even follow you through thick and thin due to the high esteem that I hold for you.

So Edward, be informed that you can be my leader, my advisor and my lover all in one. You do me proud up to the point that I have shaken off all my pride. I have exposed all of my innermost feelings to you. I can even follow you right to the ends of the earth, blindly, even with closed eyes for I trust, and know it in my heart that you are the best leader, the best lover and very best friend with my best interests at heart. You are all that I might yearn to have. I have decided to show you all my whole being by exposing to you what is in my heart and soul. I love you Edward. You now own my heart, yes you possess all the love my heart can hold and is capable of giving.

Enjoy the remainder of your day, and later a restful night. I wish for YOU to subdue any challenge that comes your way. God meant for you to be a conqueror, so be it. To me, YOU mean more than you might ever know. Edward, now I know that I love you with every fibre of my being.

Melody

#14 Melody keeps focused

June 25, 2010

Darling Edward,

Good morning. You are still asleep I suppose. I wish if I could wake you up with a morning kiss even before dawn.

I am so happy to learn that the showing of all the furniture and equipment in the building went well and that the sale will be closed today. That is good. It's a job which was well done. You are good.

It's always good to have friends whom you can count on. I am sure your friend had a nice time in St. Lucia. Thank you my love to put me first before your friends and for telling me that you can't trade me for the world. I appreciate you Ed. I also want to reassure you that you will never regret this move. You are the King in my life and I will be your loyal and devoted Queen. Here we are talking about companionship for life. I will forever remember that you traded all your good life and friends for me. I will forever be indebted to you my love. I realize what a giant step this is to you. I also know that you are basing it all on faith and trust, and love. I can never forget that. Ed, you are just my "unforgettable man".

The time we will be staying together, I will put your feelings first and foremost. Edward we will be one, the two of us will just live as one. I love, adore, admire and I will respect your decisions. I will make sure that you have all the peace that you want and that you are happy. I will do anything in my power to guarantee that your life with me will be memorable and full of peace and happiness. I will give you all the good loving and more. You will be in my loving arms. I will make sure you will feel at home since home is where you will be.

Thanks for last night. You talked to baby. I have to tell you that I became emotional about the whole thing. It's the first time that I have made her talk to someone who is part of me like you.

You will be the closest to a Dad that she will ever know. Ed, there will never be any other man in my life, ever besides you. I can guarantee you all the respect you deserve from the children and all the loving you might need from me. I adore you my love.

Good morning my love, my destiny and my lover. I wish you a great day full of all the pleasant surprises and all the desires of your heart. You are so special my darling Ed, I love you.

All my love,
Melody

#15 Ed looks at the possibility of bringing forward his Itinerary

June 26, 2010

Dear Melody,

Hello Sunshine! Good Morning my Love!!!!

Are you going to the market today? What will you be buying for me? Give me an itinerary as to what you expect me to do in a typical day in Arusha. I need a blow by blow account 6.00 am to bed time. It is your call.

I did go out this evening but didn't enjoy myself due to the weather. I left at 5.30, got back at 9.00pm. There is no joy in going out these days as I await my new life. You seem to be very happy with the new possibility of an earlier ETA and so am I.

I am still having difficulty with the song. You need to give me the instruction to download the song. I am feeling tired so I will get the power point details to you first thing tomorrow.

Baby, be good. Enjoy Saturday. Remember, I love you and will always do.

Love Always,

Ed

#16 Is Ed thinking straight?

June 25, 2010

Dear Melody,

Goodnight!

I had a great morning and as discussed over the phone it may be sooner rather than later. I could be arriving at your doorsteps at the end of July. Are you ready for that? I hope I am not pushing you. I am glad that you said it was OK and from now on we will be working at it.

I feel I am already in Arusha. Forward ever, backward never. Have you ever heard the story of the soldiers who landed on a beach belonging to the enemy and upon arrival burned the boat so there could have been no retreat? Sometimes, I wonder if I am still in my right senses. All I can say is that it is LOVE that has done this to me. I trust you and I have your commitment and you have mine. We have come to a mutually beneficial position.

Melody, enjoy the rest of the evening. I will greet you when you awake. Hopefully, you will have the final draft of the Work Ethic document to put on the PowerPoint. I don't plan to be out this evening at least at this time but I never know.

Goodnight my Love, Pleasant Dreams and sleep tight my Love!

Love Always,

Ed

#17 Melody helps Ed with his work load

June 26, 2010

Darling Ed,

Good afternoon my love.

I left home before you were awake. Baby had been invited to a party for a kid who has turned 7 years of age, Baby was the youngest. The venue was at the New Arusha Hotel.

IT WAS NICE WITH ALL THE JUMPING CASTLES BUT POOR BABY IS STILL TOO YOUNG FOR MOST OF THE FUN. However, she seemed to have been enjoying the fun as she was really excited to be with so many other children.

I was missing you so much my love. I saw the presentation and will put it on PowerPoint. I have to read your other mail. Thought I should tell you where I was first. Your love note will be following before end of the day. Have to rush to the gym for just an hour and will be back to write your mail, I miss you my darling.

I love you Edward. I hope your day has been good so far.

Till then my love,

Melody

#18 Melody assures Ed - Everything will be fine

June 26, 2010

My darling Ed,

You are just amazing. You just know how to keep me recharged with excitement. You can make me so happy Ed. You have the art of doing that. Thank you my love.

Thank you for the telephone call, I really love talking with you. So your heart is already here - right? You have programmed yourself for this place. You have just won all of my heart Ed. Indeed my darling, our hearts would be beating as one. Everything will be fine for us.

I need you home here, so please my darling - come to me. I am so lonely without you by my side. You are all that I need Ed. If you manage to come by the end of July, Darling, that would make my heart leave the ground and to go waltzing on top of the world. That would be splendid. That would be so great, to say the least. Darling, I just can't wait. Honey I need you, honest I do. What else can I say Ed, saying I miss you is an understatement? Well, at the same time I understand that you have to finalize your business deals. July would be perfect if you manage to come.

I like the story of the soldiers, burning their boat so that they could not retreat? For our love, I think I could do the same, for I am discovering that I love you with such a passion that I can't even understand. I just can't understand myself anymore. Is this love - Ed? I love you my man and that it's proving to be so hard for me to be living without you. The day we meet, I also think, the earth will come to a standstill. Even heaven would witness and record the event.

Ed, you are my hero, yes you are my champion. I even feel that you are my better half, I need you Edward.

Good night my darling.

#19 Melody apologises

June 26, 2010

Ed my love,

I am sitting on my bed writing to you. It's night time yes, and that's when I miss you the most. Today honey I am in the mood for you. I enjoy talking with you on the phone. Yes love, you are right, I should have told you where I was going at least. Oh, this won't happen again darling. I can imagine how you felt; I am so sorry my love. However, you were constantly on my mind.

This kind of loving is rare. I just can't stop thinking that we will be together soon. That is at least so comforting. This kind of feeling is too strong. My whole body is just yearning for you, for your presence and for your good loving. I just can't stop thinking how it's going to be like, when we meet and will be together, on our own. I love you Ed, yes I do and very much.

My heart is racing due to my need of you; thank you Ed for restoring me. I mean, you have managed to make me feel like a woman once more. I now feel that I need you. I feel that I need you as the man in my life. I feel that I am incomplete without you. I feel that I need to love and be loved only by you. I need to be touched by you and I am craving for your lips on mine. Oh Ed, I am in need of your loving. I feel you all over me. I feel the wave of passion sweep all over me. I think I can even be contented by just being in your arms. I think if you just wrap your arms around me, it would feel like heaven. I am imagining all sorts of things. It's so funny though, since this is not at all like me. I am overcome by you Ed.

Regarding the Arusha itinerary for you, from morning to night, I will make the rough timetable for you. Where will I start? From going to bed or from waking up? Oh let me do it tomorrow during the day for the sake of sanity. This night time is becoming a pain to me. Without you Ed, I am lost; I lose focus and am burning with loneliness and desire.

My dearest Ed, if this is not love, then there is no love at all. I have succumbed to this thing called love honey. It seems I can't help myself. I wish if you could just help me make it through the night. I can imagine that one night with you is like heaven, my love. I need you honey, Yes my love, I need you with my everything. I have set aside all my feminine pride so as to let you know that it's now too late for me to even imagine that I can do without you. You have control of my life, now I can't do without you my love. I have been made captive by your kind of love. I can never be the same again. Darling, please come and rescue me from these feelings. I am afraid that it's ONLY YOU who can.

Ed, according to my heart, you are the only one for me. You are my Prince Charming. Ed, you are but so ideal for me. I LOVE YOU my dear man, oh yes I do. It's a fact that I am burning with desire for you. Sorry I have to put it so openly. Oh Ed, I am so shy even to be saying this to you, but that is the plain truth. I am not even ashamed of myself, just imagine. What is happening to me Ed? YOU have made it happen to me. I LOVE YOU EDWARD.

Thank you for taking it a bit easy on yourself, not going out as before, as you said. Please preserve all of you for me. Please keep yourself safe for my sake.

Ed, this is some form of madness. The truth is, it's only you who can satisfy this feeling. It's only you who can make me sane again. My dearest Edward come and take my hand and run with me into the future - our future. I love the way it sounds. Come and show me how to live again. I believe in you dear Edward.

By the way, thank you my love for your morning email. You helped me make it through the day. I love the way you write to me. You make my world exciting and interesting just with your words. You make my life worthy of living. You make my life come alive and my heart pulsate with expectation. You have reshaped my life in a way which I never thought would be possible. I owe you a gift of gratitude for this wonderful feeling you give to me my love. Thank you!

Enjoy the remainder of your day and later have a very good night. Melody

#20 Love notes as a routine feature in Melody and Ed relationship

June 27, 2010

Dear Melody,

I will retire after saying Good Morning to my baby!

I will like us to continue writing love notes even when we are living together. Another thing is for us to maintain an effective Diary primarily for me and for us.

I stepped out this evening after spending all day at home to buy a few items from the Pharmacy and I picked up two of the three properties I sent you. Most people remember my business when they see me.

Well, what's new? 32 days to go. I am counting down the days. I am hoping everything works out as planned. I am keeping my eyes on the prize. I just want to be close to you. I am devoted to you. It appears that I am comfortable here, reasonable potential but yet I am prepared to leave all and run into your arms. I guess it is the challenge to start from the bottom - a new life of love and affection! It doesn't get any better, does it? My bags are mentally packed and if you get my drift you will understand it is a very light bag. It would have been great if I could have walked off the plane, meet my new family and go straight to a departmental store and buy a completely new wardrobe. That would have been great.

Is there a hot and a cold season in Tanzania? It is the wet season here as we experience regular rainfall during the hurricane season. It seems cold in South Africa based on the dress of some Anchors.

I have decided to follow your suggestion, just leave everything until I get there. Let us spend some time just enjoying the distance between us so we can cherish the togetherness when we get together. Did I hear you say we will communicate by telephone only once per day? Maybe, once per week? Can we do that? What do you say? Did I hear right????? Don't get mad at me - I love you!

I will be meeting with a Realtor at 9.00 am to give her some advice on a property she wants to buy and then I will go to my office and do some work. You would have observed that I seldom visit my office, I like working in my pyjamas and Boxer shorts. Either is very comfortable.

I planned to spend 15 minutes writing to you and ended up spending 45.

Love Always - Ed

#21 Melody expresses her love for Ed
June 27, 2010
Hello my darling,
Heya!!!!!!

Today you made me laugh darling. The way I love you, I wish if you knew. Nothing like that would ever, ever happen in my life as long as I live. When I say I love you, I mean I LOVE YOU. No other man in my life.

You are the only man in my heart and that is it. Also in my heart there is only room for one, yes only one man, that one man happens to be YOU, Edward Harris.

Oh Edward, I wish if you would get into my heart and measure how I love you. You ARE the reason why I am so excited. My life has become so exciting due to your presence in it. I love you my darling. I love you with my everything. You are at the centre of my universe. You will be the love of my life until eternity.

That is my son with me in the picture. He is on vacation till the 12th of July. His toe is a lot better. The doctors said they would remove the caste on the 3rd of July. He says it's no longer painful.

Finally, I managed to download that song. I am sure you can manage to play it now. Ed, I love you in such a way that no other man will ever have an impact on me whatsoever. So rest assured, no man for me ever. After all, I would never try to cause any pain to you my love. I just take you as part of my own body, Thank you for loving me in turn. Thank you Edward, for your willingness to start a life with me.

I have given you all of me, to have and to hold. You are ALL that I need honey. I was looking at your picture and I am more than convinced that YOU EDWARD HARRIS, you are where I end. You got everything I need. I will be the most proud woman on earth just being by your side. You just do me proud.

Edward you are my MIRACLE and you are God's gift to me. God is faithful. I prayed to God to give me somebody to love and God answered by giving you to me. I love you Edward and I pray that nothing comes between our precious love.

Ed, you will be my life companion if you really love me the way you confess to me. I will be devoted to you for life. I will forever be faithful to you darling.

Well. I hope you enjoy the football match, but always remember that someone loves you honey, more than anything in the world.

Melody

#22 Ed introduces Melody to the technique of Positive Thinking

June 30, 2010
Darling Ed,

I just read "The power of the Mastermind". What a book!!!! It's an e-book right? Can you see how catching the Title and theme are. The subject is perfect. Who does not want to get rich? So everyone would then want to think that way if that's the way to get to be rich. Wow!!

This book motivates people to develop positive thinking and faith. It's a biblical and physical truth. He also points out that birds of a feather flock together. Isn't it true that we are influenced by the people we hang out with most times? Sometimes, we end up developing same characteristics, mannerisms and traits as those of our close friends. That is where the notion that if you associate with the rich you will be rich and with the poor you will become the same.

Such a book with a topic which affects nearly everyone in society and which seems to suggest a formula to people's major want- riches, can find a market so easily. We can learn a lot from things like these, you know. It's a very interesting book if I may say. It has taught me one or two things as well just by reading it.

You just don't stop to amaze me darling. You seem to know where to get whatever information we need on the internet, no wonder why providence pointed you to someone you are very much in tune with on the net. You are just a born leader who is very positive in nature. That's a great virtue in itself.

Edward, you are a natural optimist. I like your positive attitude to life. Even the bible says, you will have what you believe. Also Jesus used to tell the people that let it be as they believed and also he even asked people whether they believed. He even told some that their faith had made them whole. Faith, positive thinking, and power of the tongue are so amazing? Our words mould our lives in a great way. It's quite an amazing and powerful weapon.

I suppose we should affirm more everyday in this life honey. It's a powerful weapon. Furthermore, good planning and putting things into action right? You can see how I am trying to catch up with your kind of thinking. L.O.L.

I understood what you said in your morning mail that I should wait for your flight schedule and then book the domestic flights in and out of Dar es Salaam. That will be done. I am actually looking forward to the event of your coming with every fibre in me. The thought of that has made me a better person in many ways. I feel great.

So, how has been your day so far? I hope you have gone over your presentation by now. Please advise on any suggestions, changes, alterations, corrections, amendments, omissions or additions? Please let me know.

Thank you for observing that I am a good helpmeet and a fantastic woman. You made me smile. Well I will strive to answer to that, yes I will try to be the best helpmeet in your life wherever I can, whenever I can. I love you Edward. I will stand by you through whatever that may come our way. I will be there for you; yes you can count on me a hundred percent.

Enjoy the remainder of your day, and later sweet dreams but never forget that someone loves you honey.

Melody

#23 Melody wants to ensure Ed is comfortable

July 1, 2010

HELLO LOVE,

I assume that you are awake now and fully rested from the fatigue of yesterday.

IT'S LUNCH TIME HERE and since morning I have been so busy with some archiving project for HQ. Thanks for the pictures which I saw first thing in the morning. Thanks for your mail which always gives me the strength to start a new day.

You look so wholesome in those pictures darling. I will have to reserve some of the compliments until the time you will be here. Oh, Edward, so you will be sending pictures to me nearly every day before you come? That's so sweet of you. How did you figure out that I am addicted to your pictures? You see what I mean when I say you seem to read my mind. You seem to know me through and through. I am amazed. Thanks then for the pictures in advance. I love you more.

I am happy for you that you had a good day yesterday. So your friends want to throw parties for you? Wow!! That's great. It shows how popular you are.

Sometimes, I feel a bit guilty that you have to leave your comfort zone, so that we can be together. I also feel as if I am being selfish but I still feel great just to know that you will be coming. I know this country is different from St. Lucia and you will need to adapt to the way of life here. I am always telling myself that I will help you adapt. You can even attend Kiswahili classes.

I will write some more soon. I can see you have beaten me to this mail.

Good morning my love. How do you feel today?

Be blessed, I love you.

Melody

#24 Ed prepares health requirements

July 2, 2010

Dear Melody,

Good Morning!

By the time you awake, it will be 29 days to go. I hope you had a pleasant night and you dreamt of me. I don't like the photo which was taken at the barber shop as I didn't pose for it. It is too ordinary but anyhow that's me, have fun. It has been a hectic day. I dropped asleep in front of the computer. I got up at 6.00 am to write my article and deal with my mails, then rush down the road to do several things, had to walk around the city as parking is a problem. The experience of sitting in a barber's chair is very relaxing. I am rested now and hope I don't have to go out tonight so I will be fresh tomorrow for my presentation.

You asked how I write, it is simply by using the same principle that you use in writing to me. Just start writing and the information flows. You and I will make a great team. I have no fear of the future. I am ready to be your mate. Don't worry about the young women, I have gone past that. I am not looking back. My future is with you. I love you! You are no more anxious than I am about our getting together. We deserve each other and are more than worthy to receive the love of God in granting us the desires of our hearts. Love is all we need and I am persuaded that we have an abundance of love enough for us and to share.

I didn't get to make a booking for my vaccination but next week wouldn't pass. I have to be fit and ready to take my journey. It is a wonderful world with beautiful people. Imagine, us meeting in Dar es Salaam for three full days. I hope you will arrange to arrive before me so that you will be at the airport to reach me or else I will be lost.

Say a special prayer for me when you awake and as soon as my presentation concludes you will receive word on how it was received. I will spend the rest of my time at the computer going over the presentation. Thank you for your efforts,

Have a great Friday. Thank God it's Friday!

Love Always - Ed

#25 Melody supports Ed

July 2, 2010

Ed, my love,

Good morning darling,

Let's hope your sleep was restful since it's our big day today.

I wish you the best in your speech darling. You will be more than fine - that I know. It's in your blood, in your genes you have the most wholesome brains with such intelligence that is not common place. We have to thank God for that. I love you more.

So there is nothing to worry about. Go and shine, as usual, for both of us. I will be with you in spirit. Edward I am so proud of you. You will do a splendid job for those teachers, I can assure you of that my love. You are the best.

Let me not disturb you a lot. I will write your love note later so that you will see it when you come back from the presentation. I just want you to remember that you have captured my heart totally. I will always love you Ed.

Good morning once more and welcome to a new day. Yes, go and do your best!!! You are loved by me, now and always.

Melody

#26 Melody is missing Ed and praying

July 2, 2010

My darling Edward,

If only you knew how I missed you today, you could have been more sympathetic with me. Do you know what it means to me to be in love? Honestly Ed, I just don't know what to do with myself. I miss you like I have never missed anyone in my life. Yes I need you, so badly. It's so funny how by just looking at your picture at the presentation I felt so aroused. Oh God, I just don't know how to tell you this. I am discovering new feelings in me. I love your pictures. You were so elegant, oh my, my!! I real liked the way you were dressed. I love you my darling.

You said 28 days? How I love to hear that. I can't stop imagining all sorts of things. Ed, I can't wait. I am excited every time I realize that you are indeed coming. Do you know that honey?

Ed, when you come I will be in Dar es Salaam already. I will be waiting for you. I just love the idea that we will be together, alone for 3 days before going to our home in Arusha.

My daughters are praying that you would really come, for they think that if you don't come, that might even kill me of a heart break. Actually, they fear that if you are not serious or if you don't mean that you love me, I might never be the same again. I tried to reassure them that you are very genuine and real. They all know that I am seriously in love, and I have given my all to this relationship. They understand that I have given all of myself, body and soul to you. These children really love you. So you can see how they are also looking forward to meet you someday soon, here at home.

You say you are ready to be my mate honey? I love to hear that. I also am ready to be your everything, for I am lost in your love. What I know for sure is, it could be very, very difficult for me to go on without you. I can give anything so as to be with you. I know and am more than convinced that we are meant for each other. This is no accident, it is destiny. I feel that you are the one for me.

Thank you for the telephone call my love. Talking with you means a lot to me. You even managed to call from where you had gone for a meeting? You are so kind. Oh Ed, I love you more my darling. I appreciate that telephone call. You are so sweet. Our baby slept as soon after our telephone conversation. How funny? I also become so restless when I haven't heard from you even for a few hours. I know the feeling. Thank you for loving me honey and all the concern you show. It all reassures me and makes me so happy.

I also am so confident of the future my love. I know that together we will make it. Together we can confront anything and succeed. I hope you reach here safely and healthy. If you have a flu/cold, don't worry, I will nurse you back to health so fast, you won't believe. At least Dar es Salaam is hot and humid so it will help a bit.

Arusha is cool. These days, it's on the cold side. Tanzania has like 2 seasons - Summer and Winter. Actually it's like Summer, Winter and Spring maybe, a very short Autumn, nothing really like in the southern hemisphere.

I hope you enjoy your meeting and the remainder of the day my love. I think it's high time I go to sleep. I think I dreamt of you last night but I forgot the dream save for the fact that it was a very good, happy and peaceful dream and you were in it. Maybe, I might dream again. How I wish if I was there to lie beside you and kiss you till you fall asleep. I am missing you terribly. It's so sad to be alone in bed. Soon we will be together my love.

I love you Ed.
Melody

#27 Ed recognizes the need for compromise

July 3, 2010

Dear Melody,

Good Morning!

It is a joy and privilege to have someone as caring as you enter my life. I feel blessed because this can only be the work of the Almighty.

I had a great meeting which ended after 6.00pm. A few options for business relations were discussed. However, I just want a quiet, rewarding life, writing books and travelling to exotic locations, living the dream.

I noted your request that in the event of change of date I should not come during the period noted. That is fine; don't bother, we will maintain our original dates. I am just as anxious to be with you as you have expressed. I can't imagine going on without you. I can see my life being very complete with you. What else can I ask for in a woman? Caring, loving, intelligent, decent, respectable, having all the virtues a man could ever hope for. You touch my heart, soul and body. I pray that nothing will come between us to prevent our dream of a lifetime together to be ruined. But God is faithful to his word and He will see us through. This is the life I always dreamed of and I can see it all coming together now. I will be faithful to my commitment to love and cherish you for the rest of my life. Your love sustains me. I never committed to a woman as I have committed to you. In all my relationships it has been about me, for the first time it is about us. I want you to seriously believe this. I love you. I want you and your family to be assured of this. I am very happy that your children are appreciative of our relationship. That is excellent news.

You challenge me every step of the way to bring out the best in me. I am through our writings a gentler person. I recognized in recent times the need to compromise and see the other person's point of view. You are very persuasive but gentle about it. We should never have reasons to be angry with each other. I will make allowance for your moods if that ever arise. Where there is love and it is sincerely expressed in the way we relate to each other, there can be no room for anger. I believe in love. Let love be our guiding principle. Can you imagine what our first twenty four hours together will be like? We should try to visualize that experience. It is an exercise that will be a bit problematic, too much emotion, so let us give it a pass. It is difficult enough already, don't let us add any more fuel to the fire that is already burning brightly.

Have a blessed day and always remember I love you!!!!

Your Darling,

Ed

#28 Ed beginning to count weekends rather than days

July 3, 2010

Dear Melody,

Good Afternoon Darling!

I am sitting here lonely for the want of attention from you, I miss your morning charm and so I want to run to you with the hope never to miss your tender touch.

Are you making a second night or are you busy catching up on weekend chores. I know how that can be. There are certain things you must do for yourself; like going to the hairdresser, shopping in the supermarket and taking time to chat with friends on the way. Saturday is for you to catch up on your lagging activities as well.

Just thinking about it, when you have your companion to take care of, are we going to be taking walks down the street, hand in hand watching at other people hustling, trying to get things done on a Saturday when it should be a day of rest? Go for breakfast at one of the better restaurants, etc.? That's the life! I want for us, to be quietly different.

How many more weekends to go? It may be more interesting to count by the weekends. I count three (3) because on the fourth I will like to be in Dar es Salaam. I will arrive on a Sunday, starting off my flight on a Saturday if there is a direct flight. That means your leave will start on a Monday. You didn't say how many days you will be taking so that I can be properly inducted. Here is the projected date of my departure in exactly 27 days from today, Saturday, 31st July, 2010. I will fly royally on British Airways.

It is a great life when you can dream and have the ability to turn dreams that are in God's will into reality. There are too many open ended statements that fail to take into consideration the essence of the statements. For today's lesson, here are two:

1. You are in the right place at the right time. However what is

important is that you must be in the right frame of mind to make the right decision.

2. Knowledge is Power but only when it is put into action.

You now have new knowledge and we are riding on a wave of excitement, joy and glorious expectations because we took those two fundamental statements into consideration and applied them. Can we both say Amen! I love you Melody. I keep praying that everything will work our fine for us so that God's purpose will be truly established in our lives.

Love always – Ed

#29 Melody imagines life with Ed

July 3, 2010

Ed my love,

Thanks my love for the telephone call. Have noticed how I am becoming so happy to the point of failing to talk, when on the phone with you? I am becoming so breathless with love. At least you will be coming soon; otherwise I could not manage to go on like this. A few more weekends to go, that's great darling.

What I spend the greater part of my nights doing is just imagining our first 24 hours together. I just don't know. What I can say is just that, I view it as one of the most important and sentimental part of our coming together.

During weekends we might be going for walks right on the outskirts of the residential area where we will be close to nature. We might opt to visit some nearby resort areas near Arusha or even chill indoors together catching up on the happenings of the week. I just love the imagining of it all.

I am also happy that in the night I will be having someone to talk to, to whisper to, to reach for and kiss and tell how I will am feeling. It's such a blessing to have a man by your side, be it during the day but mostly during those wee hours of morning. Edward, just the idea of having the privilege of getting into someone's embrace is so heavenly. Now I think I understand why God created Eve for Adam, and why Adam had to be created first. I am more than sure that Eve would not have been able to survive on her own. She could not have survived even for a week alone. You see that God understands the nature of the woman folk? If God spared Eve any period of loneliness, then he understands my loneliness better. I need you my Edward, you are my Adam, and I miss you so very much. I feel that I was made by God with you in mind, that's according to your specific needs. I love God, and I love you.

Edward, you will have all my attention and my presence when you come over. You will never miss my touch, both day and night.

Yes Ed, we can say Amen!!!! I love you too. I also feel that we are at the right place at the right time. God is in charge and He will see us through.

Enjoy your day Ed. You are always on my mind.

Melody

#30 Who initiated the relationship?

July 4, 2010

Dear Melody,

Happy Sunday!!

I hope you had a restful night and that you will take a further rest during the day to catch up to your right energy level. Tonight, I decided to take it quietly and in preparation for my trip I took some worm medicine so sleep is best after writing my love note. I drank no alcohol today since I planned on taking the medicine. I want to be super fit when I get to Arusha or should I say Dar es Salaam. I will be taking my Yellow Fever Vaccine in the new week to ensure I deal with any side effect before my departure.

Twenty seven (27) days to go before I turn my life over to my darling Melody. I have given over the worldly control of my life to you but always I know God is in charge overall. He has given you the responsibility to provide me with the comforts of this life, principally among them is LOVE. He thought us to love and once we believe on His love, he will grant us perfect love. You are the love of my life.

At this time, we are in the spirit but soon will be united in mind, body and soul. I just can't wait. Suddenly our whole world has changed. We live in a dynamic world. The only thing that is constant is change. We live in a world of miracles. We can attest to that. I don't remember, was it I who contacted you first? Or was it you! Regardless, we love each other and it would not mean much at this time. However, it is nice to know who blessed who? I think it was me. The approach most times comes from the male and you in your fine mannered, lady like nature would have been shy. But I am convinced you are not now. Melody is as bold as a lioness. Isn't she?

I will need your full address and contact numbers for immigration when I arrive in Dar es Salaam. I guess once you exit the main airport, you are in Tanzania and can access the remainder of the country. We have to keep remembering these little things.

I get so much information daily on the internet, sometimes it is overwhelming. I am going to definitely take it easy for the first few days when I get to Arusha. I have been telling you what my friends say, you have been talking with them. What do your friends say about this giant step we are about to take??????? What is your response to them? I hope they are as receptive to the idea as my friends. This is major challenge that I dealt with very simply. I guess it is because it is something I wanted to do for almost seven years, it was just a matter of time, for us the match was made in heaven. Heaven sent me an angel. Melody, I love you to the point that I trust my life in your hands. I will do anything to make you happy at all times, striving at all times to ensure happiness in our relationship. If God be for us, who could be against us and it appears this is something that your kids are in favour of, even Baby.

As another week dawns, it is my hope that the way forward becomes clearer and everything works together for good. I love you honey. You mean everything in the world to me. Love has truly found its way in our hearts and our lives. God bless you. Have a blessed Sunday and remember always I love you!

Your Darling,
Ed

#31 Melody informs Ed about the Zimbabwean Shona Custom
July 4, 2010
Darling Ed,

You are still asleep but here it's already morning. My night was fine, but you are right, I think I can do with some more sleep.

About airlines, you can travel with KLM instead. What they are saying about your using Precision Airline from Kilimanjaro is not correct since Kilimanjaro Airport is just an hour's drive to Arusha. There is no need to reach Kilimanjaro first since you can alight in Dar es Salaam. We need to have some time to ourselves love, to get acquainted right? It's so lovely to hear that you are preparing for your journey to us. That makes me go on. It's now 27 days to go. That is super.

You want to know who started writing first. Isn't that funny Ed? Firstly, I got a letter from the website telling me that you had put me as your favourite. Then I followed the link to your profile which I then read. After that I wrote through them saying I was happy that you had chosen me as a favourite. Then I reciprocated to make you my favourite. I think I commented how good your profile was. You then wrote back to me saying you also liked my profile too and would like us to communicate. Then we exchanged private email addresses and we started communicating.

Ed, you are so different from anyone I know. I just loved you from the word go. I liked the way you are in your pictures; you are just amazing and unforgettable in every way. At the moment, I am very much aware of the fact that I can't stop loving you. I can't love again somehow.

You ask about my friends? I have not told most of my friends save those at work. Friends from my work are finding it very interesting. They are very supportive. I told one of my nephews who is in Zimbabwe and he said it was cool but should not forget to do the traditional bit of making sure you pay the dowry for me. Isn't that funny? That's done in order for parents and big brothers to bless you. It's a Zimbabwean Shona custom. It's observed in most parts of Africa, the bride's prize, lobola or dowry. After that people can go to the courts, or church to be officially married. If I tell my brothers and sister that I have found a life mate they may want us to be united either traditionally or in a civil court. Overall, so far people seem surprised but very supportive, with many asking how we met.

Your coming is just a Dream come true my darling. You are my Miracle and I treasure you so much. I will give you all the loving I am capable of giving. Yes love, all of it, with no reservation.

You made me laugh, for you said Melody is a lioness. Am I, or a tigress? The thing is I am a harmless animal, which ever you choose but a very passionate one. My problem is I love unto madness. When I love, I really love.

Let me go now to see someone who came from England and brought a parcel for me from one of my daughters. When I come back, I will write properly. I just wanted you to see my note first when you wake up.

Edward, you are my all. Welcome to Sunday. I wish your Sunday to be full of blessings and peace. Have a nice day my love. You mean the world to me honey.

Melody

#32 Ed agrees to the Dowry
July 4, 2010

Happy Sunday! Although by the time you open this email the day would have been well advanced. However, enjoy what is left of it. I went out to take a guy to weed some grass for a friend of mine. I am going out in a while to look at a few properties this morning. I have a meeting at 4.00pm. Not bad for a Sunday.

This week I am reaching for the unreachable star. It is getting closer to my date of departure and am I excited. I just want to be close to you. We are dreaming it now but will soon live it. The words we exchange are major blocks in building our future relationship.

I hope you received lots of goodies from your daughter. So we have daughters with identical name.

I am happy for your recollection of our introductory communication because that is very important for our anniversary and all that in the future.

If I have to catch a train from Gatwick to Heathrow I am only going to come with one suitcase. It seems as though I will have to arrange for my son to post my personal effects left behind. Regarding which airline I use that will be worked out to our satisfaction. We need a cooling off period in Dar es Salaam before we get home. We need to be by ourselves to enjoy the first 72 hours. I quite understand your position. We don't want any eyes on us. We must be free to do whatever we wish to do whenever we wish. That's Freedom. I guess you are after total Freedom. I love you!

The medicine worked well, even my tummy is flat. I am trying to get in shape as I will want to be alert. One thing I must caution you about is when I am up and about I don't get tired. My friends normally sleep on me. They can't hold out on the 4.00 am parties. So be ready!

I do have some challenges now to do everything that needs to be done. Time is not on my side. I even need to get my Guyana passport. I have a brand new Saint Lucian passport. It would be great for me to get my US and European Visas before I leave. Don't panic, with or without them I am leaving here for Arusha on Saturday 31st July, 2010. Only God can change that.

I know everything about dowry. I have Indian blood running through my veins. Black people apply it in the reverse. It is the girl's parents who have to come up with the dowry. Don't worry. I will pay anything for a woman of your intelligence and warmth. You are the light in my world. I expect that Miracles will be manifested all around us with every step we take. I am in search of peace and love. I want to be in harmony with God and my mate - a winning combination. The latter has eluded me. I love what I am experiencing in our relationship. I love you. Our exchanges have been truly rewarding. I love you and I trust you. I wish the very best for us.

Love always – Ed

#33 Melody expresses her inner desires for Ed
July 5, 2010

I am not sure whether you have received the whole of this mail or just a bit because when I tried to see if it had been sent, I saw it reflecting just a quarter of the whole message. I will try to remember all that I had written and send it again. Internet can disappoint sometimes.

My darling Edward,

You know what honey, it's done and you have done it. You have hit the mark and more. This is just something else. You have won me and more. I LOVE YOU DARLING Ed.

I am more than sure now, YOU are the ONE. You are the man for me, no two ways about it. It's crystal clear my love. Thank you for being the kind of man you have been to me so far. I love what you are like. I love the way you are. You are man as a man should be according to me. I love the way you sound on the phone, the way you relate to my heart and soul and the way you just converse with me. You are a proper man. Thank you for having been born a male. Only the above is reflecting

47

as the small part which has been sent. I wonder whether I will write it exactly as before.

I had said I noticed that you have lost some weight somehow. So you are preparing for me so that you can satisfy all my needs? That's so sweet of you honey. I love the FREEDOM idea of spending 72 hours on our own, away from the children. But when we get to Arusha and the children get acquainted with you, they should understand that we need time for each other. They will have to understand that and give us their blessing for those moments we should be only the two of us. Ed, every part of my body is crying out for you. To me you are all that represents male to my senses; I am dying to be with you. Those hours we will be together will carry great sentiments in our lives. I need you Ed. I am on fire for you even as I am writing this note. I am trying to maintain some sanity since I know that every day that passes brings your arrival in Dar es Salaam closer. I LOVE YOU MY DARLING.

So your son will have to ship your shelves and some things right? That is a good idea. It is interesting that our daughters have the same name. Isn't that something my love?

So you know the dowry stuff? Yes the Indians do it the opposite of the African way. So you are prepared to do that? Oh darling thanks for that. Just by agreeing to that, you have proven that you love me so much; In essence it should be just any reasonable amount which acts as a love token. Edward, I love you even more. It's just the way you show commitment to the relationship.

Darling, whatever part of our lives that might have eluded us, we will relive it and make up for it with the abundance that we will enjoy. I love you, and will cherish you for as long as I live, every fibre within me is yearning for you. Darling I am waiting for you to come and give me some demonstration of love. You will lead in that respect. You will love me as your woman. We will explore each other and get to know what pleases each of us the most. You will also get to know what this African mate of yours is made of. I will get to know YOU as my man who satisfies my every need. We will explore all the avenues of satisfying each other my love. Ed, right now I am on fire for your loving. Darling, I can feel love in its entirety. Oh God, Ed, I just don't know how those initial hours together would be like for I need you badly.

If I have duplicated this note because it looked like it had not been sent, then it should show you how intense the feelings I have for you are. Its madness, but I would rather be mad for you. You mean the world to me darling.

So darling, enjoy the remainder of the day and later have a good and peaceful night. You are my everything Ed.

Melody

#34 Melody clears the decks

July 6, 2010

Darling Ed,

How has been your day so far?

Mine has been so full of my analysis of my life. I have been taking stock of whatever might have happened in my life before and making resolutions. I am sure the episode of yesterday has made me stop and analyze how far our relationship has been progressing.

What I have discovered is that we are far advanced with this relationship. A lot has happened so far and as far as I am concerned, there can be no retreat. I remembered the story you told me about the soldiers who burned their boat as soon as they had landed all in an attempt to make sure there was no going back.

So I have reached that point now. I think it's high time for me to burn all the bridges, or burn all my boats. What I mean is, there is no more going back. I am contented with you and we are moving forward.

I just wish to tell you that I feel like shouting it from house top that I am taken, yes, that " I AM NOW TAKEN BY EDWARD HARRIS".

Honey, do you remember asking me whether I had gotten many responses from the website where we met? Do you remember what I told you? I am sure I told you that I did get loads of responses but only later to discover that most of the people there were not real, they were either, fake, married, liars or all in one. It is amazing how disrespectful some can be.

I just want to tell you that I will never visit any such sites ever again. Also if there could have had one or two people who had continued writing to me on a casual note, as even just on a friendly basis after they had been discovered to be very married, yet they could have confessed to

49

be single, I am going to stop anyone ever writing to me, no matter how innocent it might have seemed to be. I want to remain with ONLY you, on my mailing list. I want to delete anything with relevance to any pen friends I might have exchanged mail with. I just don't want anything to do with anyone else other than YOU Edward Harris anymore. So I am going to write to all of them and inform them that I have met my match now and there is no going back. Someone whom I discovered to have been very married and living with his family and wife in South Africa had opted to keep on writing to me just as a friend and nothing else. I just have to write to him and tell him that the innocent friendship has to stop since I am now taken. I feel it's only proper Ed. That is what I am going to do. The website keeps on sending mail of who made me their favourite, so I think it's my obligation as well to just let them know that I have found my match and I don't need their help anymore.

I just want to extricate myself from unnecessary people. There is no more need to entertain any friends of the opposite sex who might have had intentions of me being their date. That would be very wrong and might bring complications later. Your coming to be with me is a giant step in both our lives so I must do all things as if I am already married to you. I have to do things properly. I don't think there is anyone who might be hurt by this since I had made it clear to whosoever that I would not date a married man living with his family.

Ed, I want to remain free for you. I want to have ONLY YOU as my lover, friend, confidante and everything. You should stand for everything I need in a man. You should be the only one who matters in my life. I don't believe in sharing, it is wrong and evil. So let me make sure that no one will ever write to me again as either a friend or whatever, they might want to term it.

Ed, I would even want Heaven to witness that today I have declared having been entirely taken by you. I love you my darling with my everything. I mean this from the bottom of my heart. If you have any further questions, you might want me to clarify for you, please be my guest darling. You are the only man who has managed to reach the innermost part of my heart. Whatever could have been or aspired to be in my life is now history and it should remain so.

Darling I can't wait for Dar es Salaam. I miss you badly. I also want to inform my two brothers, sister and any relative who matters that I am deeply in love with you. Edward, I will be all yours. I will be so proud to be your mate. I can only see you in my life, from now on. Please remember this always. I can't give up the love we now share for anything in the world.

Enjoy the rest of your day. I love you.

Melody

#35 Ed putting everything in order for his trip

July 8, 2010

Dearest Melody,

Good Morning! I wish you a great day. Enjoy!

It was a hectic day, I sent you the results. I have not rested as yet. I am committed to fulfill my duty to write to you before I sleep, although I am very tired. I will awake early to write my article. You absconded from your responsibility last evening and left me to go to bed without my love note and goodnight kiss. That isn't fair but there must be a reason. I guess it was a power blackout. That's the problem of developing countries. I went through that in Guyana, my homeland so I can live with it. The generator will be helpful but you must ensure that your workers take it off every time before adding fuel or else it is likely to blow up.

Twenty three (23) days to go and I can't wait. Everything seems to be working fine financially and I am just praying for good fortune to attend me. I had a major development this afternoon which could bring us some real joy. Keep praying with me, our prayers are being answered one at a time. I am comfortable with the developments.

All my lose ends are coming together now and I will be OK. So baby it looks good. I will not work in the nights as I do now, the evenings and nights are for you. Computers will be turned off as soon as you enter the door to make sure we relax, look at TV or play music or go out to dinners. Don't believe I will be pressuring you with any of my work when you come home from work, not to work. We are going to live one of the most carefree lives. I have learnt the art of living like a millionaire with little or no money. There is a method to that. I will teach you how.

Well darling the seriousness of the day wants to linger as you would have noted I did not once mention I Love You! We made the decision regarding the utilization of the word LOVE which will keep us together in harmony. Melody, I love you and that's a TRUTH. I love you more than words can say. I feel like squeezing you and have you rest your head on my breast. I will purchase a set of perfumes especially for our evening get together. Oh I am dreaming. This will be the greatest love of all. Do you have duty free shops in Arusha where foreigners can buy Duty free? If yes, are they expensive? It is said when you ask the price, you just can't afford. We will strive to achieve Financial and Time Freedom in the shortest possible time!

I finally got through to the Health Centre and the Hospital. I will go to the Health Centre. The nurse informed me that I will have to take the vaccine ten days before I travel and I will have to walk with Malaria tablets. You did not tell me that. Make sure I know everything I need to know well in advance so there could be no surprises such as the need for the vaccine ten days before travel.

I am living very quietly over the past few days, not going out in the evenings, not drinking, just thinking about what it will be like for me in Arusha. I am really dreaming and praying that everything will work out all right.

Well my love, I pray that you awake with my love manifested all over your face. I mean that I wish you will awake smiling. Have a blessed day. Every day when leaving home take a photo for me.

You are my Miracle! I love you!

Ed

#36 Melody wrestles with her emotions

July 8, 2010

Heya!!!

I could only read your love note until just now. I could only browse it in the morning. That is how hectic this place has been.

I am known to be an ever smiling person here but today, no, I have one of my sternest faces ever. That Sunday best smile has vanished. L.O.L. It's so funny, isn't it? Sorry for all this whining and carrying on. I am just not happy for it has deprived me of the time to respond to your mail in time.

Yesterday the electricity had come back exactly after the 20 minutes as they had specified, but only to go out again around 8:00 pm. At least we were having some takeaway. We have some Chinese restaurants here. We also have duty free shops for the UN families and some NGO organizations. They are slightly cheaper but sometimes they won't have everything. At least they are there.

I can tell how busy you are. Your work can be very stressful I know and I sympathize. It's good to know that you will be doing something less stressful here. I am so excited for your promise of having time for me when here. You said all work will stop as soon as I get home from work. That's wonderful news my love.

Edward, I am getting into the mood for you now. This squeezing and resting, on your breast, is just getting the better of me. It's so amazing how you are managing to have this kind of effect on me whilst you are thousands of miles away. I honestly wonder what will happen to me in Dar es Salaam when you will be here in person. Goodness knows.

I am so comforted to know that at least things are moving on your side. I can see all the documents that you are forwarding to me concerning the progress with regard to the listed properties. Let us continue standing on faith and wait for God to do the best for us. One way or the other, God will definitely see us through. I believe in that. Good fortune should be on its way to you just now. So you will be fine. Yes things will all be fine.

It's a good thing you are going to the health centre. Oh, about the malaria prevention medication? Well I just thought you could take the medication as soon as you get here. Now its winter and malaria is not as rife. After all we got mosquito repellent creams and mosquito nets virtually everywhere, including in all good hotels so that is not a problem. Don't worry about that. If the Health Centre gives you the preventative tablets, fine. When you are here you can still take. The best medication that Tanzania has is for Malaria, so things are under control.

It's good to know that you have at least experienced power cuts in Guyana. We will be fine I suppose. The generator should be in place soon. What is, actually missing in my life is YOU. Besides that, anything else is so trivial.

You said 23 days? Life is good and God is so good. To say I am happy is just an understatement.

I LOVE YOU EDWARD HARRIS. I have started smiling and feeling so cheerful in spite of my earlier complaints of being overworked here. You just brighten my life Eddie. Man, you are loved in such a way that you might never realize possible - you know? It's just amazing that it's possible that I am loving you, and feeling for you this way, that I can feel so incomplete when I am without you. My life seems to be so empty and meaningless with you being so far away. It's just incredible. It's so surprising and frightening at the same time. How did this come to be? How can it also feel so natural? How come it feels like a jigsaw puzzle falling into place, yes YOU AND ME? THAT, REALLY DEFEATS ME.

Ed, YOU HAVE REALLY CONQUERED ALL THAT IS WITHIN ME. SHOULD I SAY, I AM SUBDUED BY YOUR LOVE? I really am addicted to you. Do you know, or do you? I am discovering how I can no longer do without you, and your love. Please honey, come home. I will be waiting for you. I can do anything for your love, and I mean it darling.

You just blow me away. You made me laugh a lot about the dowry. It's so insignificant you know. It's just a symbol. Do you want to know what history says people used to do in Africa when the groom could not raise the dowry soon enough and they were so much in love as you and me? I hear that they could present the in-laws with a little bottle of snuff, yes ground tobacco to stand as a promise that they would pay at a later date. So funny, so you see, anything can happen when two people are in love. Some used to elope with their lovers, go in hiding, only to come out when they could meet their obligation. It's amazing how people could go to any length for love. Also, we can do anything for our love. I also can feel it that all will be well with us. We will be together no matter what and we will make our life a happy one.

It's very important that you have toned down a bit in your going out. You need to preserve all the energies for the task before you and eventually the trip to Africa, your motherland. Well it's going to be your home my love. Please remember that our home is not a complete home without you in it. There is need for you here. Your absence is being felt way too much.

In 30 minutes time I will be on my way home.

At the moment I have been told that electricity has been restored so I hope to write you some more, after everyone has retired to bed and the environment would be quiet and peaceful, allowing my thoughts to flow and then giving more room for me to express my inner feelings without any reservation.

I love you Ed. I miss you. Actually I hunger for your love.

Melody

#37 Melody feels their love is mutual

July 8, 2010

Ed my love,

Thank you for the phone call. There is nothing as good as hearing your voice on the phone. The only problem is it puts me in the mood for you. Just like now, I remain battling with all forms of emotions. I feel that I could do with your arms around me. I feel like I want your touch, your cares. I feel that I want to be kissed and hear your whisper in my ear. I feel that I want to feel your breath on my face. Ed, I would have liked to feel your heartbeat next to mine.

Night time is something else. I feel lonely and I miss you beside me. I miss being talked to. I love the way you talk my love. Edward, it's just apparent how I can't function without you. I need to be fulfilled by you. I could give anything, just to be close to you. I know that you also love me the way I love you. Edward, where are you my love?

It's so unbelievable how I feel so incomplete without you. I feel so unfulfilled with you so far away darling. At least we can now say 22 days to go. That alone eases the tension and stress. I need you with me Edward. Come and grace my life. I feel that you belong with me where ever I am. You are my number one desire. I LOVE YOU EDWARD.

I am now listening to the song that I dedicated to you "Distance and Time" by Alicia Keys. Yes no matter how far you are, no matter how long it will take you. I will be waiting.

From tomorrow, I will have a picture taken every day that I will be forwarding to you on a daily basis. Sometimes, I just feel so lost and lonely even in a room full of people. Good God this love is killing me softly. I am hungry for your love. I just know that there is only one like you Ed. You are all that I am living for. Can't you see it's only you who makes me feel this way? Ed, you are my only reality, can you see that Ed. You are my first and last for there is no way God could have made two of you - no. You are my only reality though we are separated by distance and time.

Darling, enjoy the rest of your day. I wish for you only the best of blessings and later may you have a peaceful and restful night so as to meet the challenges of the coming day. You are always on my mind and my heart is yearning just for you. I love you and will forever do.

Edward you will be my treasure forever.

Melody

#38 Melody looks forward to Ed's Love Notes

July 9, 2010

Darling Edward,

Good evening my darling.

It's always nice to speak with you. Thanks for calling, you are so sweet Ed. I can tell that you are too busy darling. I sympathise with you. Pole sana honey.

I love the photos but they can't equal your love notes. I love your writing. I actually look forward to your love notes in a way you will never know darling. I love you so very much for those love notes you mail to me. It's like your heart it communicating directly with mine. The intimacy, of these notes is of the highest degree. They cannot be compared to anything. I feel you through those notes. Your photos are great. To me they portray you alright but, your love notes speak volumes. I love you darling!

Edward, I am in love with you and it looks like I just can't help myself. I am looking forward to your coming like I have never done with anything in my life ever before. I CAN'T IMAGINE THE JOY I WILL FEEL WHEN YOU ARRIVE IN DAR es SALAAM MY DARLING.

Edward, I just know that it's only you I need forever. I just don't know what I should say to let you know exactly how I feel for you. Words seem not to be enough.

Do you want me to confess my darling? I am in tears whilst writing this note. The feeling is too much; I just feel what I can't explain. I am not sad but I am overcome by your love. I miss you Edward.

You were saying it looks like forces or happenings seem to be trying to prevent you from coming to Arusha. Darling, the truth is that, I will wait for you no matter how long it might take for you to come to me. Yes, I will be waiting. However, I feel confident that you are coming no matter what. I believe that, with all that is within me.

Edward, every single day my love for you keeps on growing more and more. You are the joy of my life honey. It's very true that I can't live this life without you anymore. That is the truth, though it might sound strange. Darling come and sail with me on the oceans of love.

My mind is with you. I am dreaming that YOU will come and sail away with me. I can picture you with me at my side. I need you more than all those women who are trying to entice you. I picture you sleeping beside me darling. It's only you who can satisfy my every desire. It's only you Edward whom I need. Do you know that in my life I had never cried for a man? For you Edward, I am crying. My heart is bleeding for your companionship. I am failing to understand myself anymore. Why and how is this happening to me my love? How can this be possible? I am not even ashamed to let you know that I am shedding tears for you. I am praying for your arrival. Oh what perfect timing for you to have made this call. I have been drowning in my tears for you.

I love you darling. I will send this note just now and perhaps write another one. I am subdued by your love. Thank you my darling. I love you so very much Edward.

Melody

#39 Melody claims that their relationship was established by an Angel

July 10, 2010

Darling,

Welcome back. I hope all went well. YOU MUST KNOW THAT I LOVE YOU, my love. Darling you are always on my mind. Do you know that it's morning here? It's exactly 1:20 am and I am still awake, and thinking of you. I am looking at one of your pictures. Those eyes of yours will surely kill me with desire. I love your eyes. I love your mouth I am missing your embrace. Oh my darling, Edward you are my love.

You said something about your moustache? I could give anything just to feel it with my mouth. It's all about our love, so shall it be forever, never ending. After all is said and done I will still keep on loving you till eternity.

Darling, on the day that I found you, there must have been an angel by my side who led me to you. Definitely something heavenly must have led me to you. That angel must also have preached to you first. When I was led to you I knew that it was you. I know the day I will see you, you will give me the kiss of life. Actually, I bless the day I found you. Darling it's all about our love. I believe it will never end. After all this time I have been waiting for you, the time I will set my eyes on you, I will just give you all the love I am capable of giving. Even now darling, my heart is beating fast darling. I am all yours Edward.

Your love is the sweetest gift that only the heavens can bestow. I am asking God that he should always keep you protected. Your love shines in my life like morning, darling. You are proving to be my daybreak. I love you so much Edward. I just can't carry on without you my darling. I am missing you so very much right now. I need you my love.

I am now hanging on every word you say. You are my hope.

Have the best of the remainder of your day and later a restful night.

Edward, you mean the world to me.

Melody

#40 Melody confesses – Love is a wonderful feeling
July 11, 2010
Edward,

I am sitting on my bed thinking of you darling. Love is such a wonderful feeling. Edward, you are such a wonder in my life. It's so good that we are in love. Love is such a wonderful feeling.

You are my dream come true. You make my life so complete and worthy of living. You stand for everything good in this world. Yes, I adore you. You are ALL that matters in this world to me. Honey, honey, honey, Umhm, you are proving to be my reason for living. I will love you till the day I die.

Edward, are you aware that you are the reason that I can't sleep early? I need you so very much that at times I just spend long moments just looking at your picture and imagining a lot and experiencing a lot of emotions passing through me. Please come to my rescue for I am falling more in love with you.

Darling, I wish if you could experience exactly these same feeling

I feel for you. This feeling is so new, wonderful and painful at times. You have now become my new definition of happiness. Believe it or not, you are the reason that I can smile and cry at the same time. I just love you my man.

Thank you, Ed, for the late telephone call. I love you more for it. I have been going through all your mail to me. I just love everything about you. You write what reaches my inner being. You have managed to capture my heart and all the love therein. You have managed to make me all your own. You have written all my feelings, and mingled them with yours to an extent that I can't distinguish between my love and yours. I feel the oneness between the two of us as inseparable.

Your love notes are a symphony of love. Your letters are a love song to my soul. The way you express your love to me is just like the words turn into an instrument that caresses me up to a point whereby I can't help myself but to surrender all of me to you, to have and to hold.

I have fallen into your love net Ed, and I am captured willingly and don't even wish, let alone struggle to get out of your tentacles of love. I have become a very willing captive. Please Ed, keep on tying me around your heart that is where I would like to belong forever. Edward, you have made me understand myself even more than I ever did before. You bring the better of me into the open that it's even surprising to me.

You display the mystery of love and portray it to me with such clarity and colourful meaning. I just manage to see ONLY you in the arena of love. You have become so real to me with such clarity that the eyes of my heart can behold you. Your love, Edward is so sweet and appeals to all my love senses in a way that surpasses anything tangible in this world. Your love is so tangible that it has managed to cushion all the abnormalities, conceal all bruises, heal all wounds that are supposed to have been and even cover all imperfections that I might have experienced in life and could have blinded me from the reality that such LOVE still exists in this wide wonderful world that you have brought to existence in my life. Where did you originate from Edward, and what calibre of good forces thrusted you into my world? Welcome to my world my darling, beloved Edward.

In your love, in your words, I see the perfection that Father God had when he created man in the garden. Yes God acknowledged that it was good, so do I Edward. You to me are the representation of that, which God termed as GOOD, soon after inspecting His work of art in the Garden of Eden.

Darling I love you and forever will do. Please darling, add more of the glue of your love so that I can never ever be separated from you and your good loving. I need you more and more as each day comes into being. You are my soul mate Eddie, and it's only you that I will ever need.

It's only you I will ever see in the environs of love. I miss you so much my love. My lips are missing your lips in the passion of a kiss. My body is crying for your embrace, my heart is yearning to feel your heartbeat in unison with its own throb next to it and my eyes are dying to see the only person I love so much. Edward I believe in OUR love but most of all, I believe in you. I am hanging on every word that you write to me. It's very true and goes without saying that, your pen is mightier than a sword for you have subdued me through and through. You have made me a willing captive of your sweet love.

At the moment we are so far apart and writing is all the weaponry that we have to express all these insurmountable feelings within our loving hearts. We might be promising a lot at the moment but that is all what we can do for now. Ed, I will never leave you lonely ever. I would never stop loving you for this kind of loving is forever. Edward I will never do anything to hurt you or your feelings.

Even though we are still far apart, I somehow feel that we share our lives together as one. I hope this expresses what I feel for now. I will forever stand by you my darling Ed. Yes, I will love you until the end of time. I LOVE YOU EDWARD HARRIS.

I wish you a safe drive back home. Enjoy the remainder of your day, experience a peaceful and yet restful night. Please take very good care of yourself, for now you are the world to me. Yes, someone in Arusha loves you honey, more than anything in the world. Good night my love,

Melody

#41 Ed confesses – his search has ended

July 10, 2010
Dear Melody,
Happy Saturday!

It was very thoughtful of you to call me this morning. You made my day. I very much appreciate this gesture on your part. Actually you know you are always on my mind. I go to sleep and wake up with you on my mind. You are everything to me. You are the breath I breathe. I pray that our love will remain as the first day we entered into this relationship until the end of time. Together, once we maintain our love already established from this distance, we are destined to be big winners in our love relations. We are going to be stars in our own movie.

I love you and look forward with my whole being to the day when we will meet in the arrival hall of Dar es Salaam airport and embrace each other. Just 20 days to go. This will be the longest month in our lives. Don't worry; we will be together and very soon.

I am going to the South shortly. Will call you later in the evening and we will communicate via SKYPE once my son is available.

Please call me always on my cell phone, I am available to the world 24 hours a day and it is near me even when I am in the bathroom. It is hectic, my phone keeps ringing all the time and I treat every call as important as I am always expecting a deal to come through the phone as I only use my cell # on my business cards.

I love you honey, you mean everything to me. My search has ended. You are the perfect one for me. You have revealed your entire world to me and I am very happy with what I see and feel. This is no game, this is very serious. I am fully convinced that you are sincere and will want to make this love we share work for both of us.

Love,
Ed

#42 Melody expresses her deep devotion for Ed

July 13, 2010
Hello, Ed,

I have seen the Investment Opportunity you sent to me. Eh, eh, that is something – dining in the sky? It's the first time for me to hear of such a business venture. Oh God, people are so resourceful, I tell you. People can just surprise you by how creative they can be in order to survive in the business world. Isn't this amazing? Well I know that you are the expert in such business endeavours and you know what the cash flow could be like when such is involved. This is really new, it's just something, I mean the idea of the whole thing. I suppose, whoever thought of such first, must have really wanted to come up with a brand new and different idea from the most common and usual businesses of everyday. Do you think investors in St. Lucia will buy it? By consulting you, it shows me that they know you in those business circles. You just amaze me Ed.

Arusha will be so different from what you are accustomed to in St Lucia. I will have to pray to God that you will manage to adapt to this completely new environment honey.

So, tell me, how has your day been so far? My working day is coming to an end. I will be going home soon darling. I am at the front desk now. A colleague has lost his wife. It's sad. Some have gone to the funeral. I had to remain finalizing the deadlines here. I think that was the best for me.

Even though I was all that busy, there was no moment that passed without me thinking of you. I am surprising myself all the time with the amount of love I feel for you darling. It is rare and something so new to me. Sometimes, I even think that I am dreaming. I imagine that I am having a fantastic dream and I even fear that I might wake up and only to discover that I would have been just dreaming. I always pray to God that he will make this beautiful dream of mine become reality. I would love to dream this dream forever darling. Indeed it's like a fairytale. I still would want to remain in this world of my fairytale. I love you so very much Ed. Thank you my darling for making me dream like this. I also believe that with your magic wand, you will also be able to keep me dreaming and eventually turn it into reality. Will you do this for me love?

Your love appeals to my love senses like nothing else I have ever heard or experienced. Edward you are a great artist of love. You are a great author of love. You have written volumes of love and embedded them into my once empty heart and filled the void which was there. You are capable of creating love were there was nothing. My heart was so empty and barren to love. Your heart managed to shower and fill up my dry heart which was like a desert devoid of love and feeling. You have authored love into my life. You have drawn such colourful volumes of love in my once plain white paper type of life.

Edward you now stand for a lot of meaning in my life. From afar, you have managed to bring all my once dormant feelings to life. What will I do if you just try to stop whatever you have done and are still doing to me? Promise me my love that you will remain real to me. Promise me that you will perpetuate this dream for me. Promise me please that you will stay with me in this fairytale love environment you have created. That is all what I am asking from you my darling man. Will you do that for me? Will you manage to keep on answering whenever I call your name Edward? Do you promise to be always there for me darling?

Sometimes, I wonder whether all this would be possible, considering that when you come over here, the only thing you will find is just my unfailing love. It's true darling that your world and the one I live in are rather different. So will my love be enough for you? I mean just my love and your computer? Will you be contented with me darling? Will you be satisfied with me and your writing only? I want to believe that Edward. I want to know that you won't ever regret having left all and opted for me instead. I know God is able to make us feel contented with each other, and HE will satisfy our heart's desires. Let us just keep on praying and affirming, agreeing with God in everything. Since God is the author of everything, He will make whatever YOU are authoring in our lives come to life for both our contentment and enjoyment. God will bless us with all HIS intended abundance as He intended for us even before we knew we would ever meet. I LOVE YOU EDWARD HARRIS, and God is my witness.

Oh, oh, can you believe this, that its 15 minutes after home time? I started thinking of you and got to writing until I forgot time. What kind of spell is this my love? What I know beyond any reasonable doubt is the FACT that I love you with all my heart Edward darling.

I think I should mail this for now and then will write a bit more for you before I sleep. You are the love of my life Edward and you will forever be. Edward, you have managed, against all odds to compose a love song in my once quiet and uneventful type of life.

Melody

#43 Ed sees Melody as a woman with many moods
July 13, 2010
Dear Melody.

I am lost without you this morning.

I am gone. I don't remember last night I am too much into the future, only 18 days to go. Your pictures were great. With every photo you look different. Woman of many moods, I can guess romantically what type of emotions will come out.

Love Ed

#44 Ed is pleased with the progress of the relationship
July 14, 2010
Dear Melody,
Good Morning!

Hope you had an enjoyable and restful night and have awakened to a best day of the rest of your life. I blessed the day I found you, I want to place my arms around you and so I beg you, let it be me. That's my version. I truly love you darling. As I write this letter I feel the touch of ecstasy. I am so satisfied with you and can only pray for the fulfillment of our dream. Our wait will end soon. Oh Happy Day!!! Are you going to run to me? I have decided to dress in a way you wouldn't recognize me. So I will walk pass you and you wouldn't realize until you turn around having felt the power of my presence.

Darling as I write this love note, I am smiling away, just feel good, just being in love with a woman who is resting peacefully. I can see her lying there in perfect satisfaction and open arms. This has got to be ordained in heaven. Oh what a joy! What a wonderful world? I am saying to myself right now. What a wonderful world. Seventeen Days to Go before I board the plane and on my way to Tanzania to begin my new life. I will have you speak with my Attorney one day when I am in her office.

I am tired. I worked hard tonight but it is worth it. My friends will remember me long after I am gone. I work hard for them whenever they request my assistance. I stayed up to finish the Press Release. It must go out for tomorrow's deadline. I sent you a copy earlier.

Thank you for your love note. I am really thankful for your commitment in doing the things that make me happy. I love you honey. I really enjoy your writings. You are wonderful, you are so sincere. Heaven must be missing an angel. We must not stop writing to each other even when we are together. Writing gives greater meaning to your thoughts. Writing commits you to action. Talking is easy but writing is a mighty act and if you write in the spirit of love it cannot be erased. It will stand before God who is ever righteous and just.

Do you have massage therapists, good doctors, dentists and eye specialists in your State? Generally what is the state of the medical services? I was hospitalized once in my life and used to get a few colds per year. In the past year I didn't catch a single cold. I am doing fair health wise, blood pressure is excellent, blood sugar normal, mostly under 100 and cholesterol just over 200 got to get that down. At the moment, I eat and drink everything I want to but I will have to make some adjustments. Let it be known I don't eat anything with feathers; I don't like lamb, except when bar-b-qued.

There are a few things I will pay attention to when I turn the new page in my life by submitting to your love and direction. I will be obedient to your command. I need to exercise, get a massage once weekly, and eat right so I can be all that you expect of a lovable and gentle man.

Well darling I still have work to do on my computer. I love you honey, enjoy your day. God loves you and so do I.

Eddie, your Darling.

#45 Melody declares – we belong to each other

July 15, 2010
Dear Edward,

I can try to imagine how busy you are. Also the fact that you are trying to make sure you tie all the loose ends of your business and any routine activities before you come. To make matters worse, you are in the middle of a lot activities at the moment. I feel for you darling. Pole sana. I just believe that here, you will find time to rest and relax.

Darling, I am sitting on this bed again, alone and thinking of you. Oh how I miss you my love. It's a good thing that you are trying to make our dream come true. I love you.

Somehow, I have started to imagine everything about you and its making my imagination run away with me. So you should just know that I am in the mood for you. Oh darling Ed, I am falling more in love with you. My heart is with you wherever you are. I miss your arms around me. Edward, I wish if you could feel me just now, for I am in the mood for your love. I need you, need you, need you, sweetheart.

I feel so bad that I missed you on Radio. I have to stay awake until midnight for your sake darling; I really want to listen to your voice on radio. I usually sleep late, so today won't make much of a difference. So I am going to listen. When it's late, internet improves. Big sister and I have been listening to Radio St. Lucia and we ended up dancing to the reggae music which was being played.

Ed, Ed, Oh darling I need you right now. I have to wait for you. Oh God, the feelings have become even stronger. The knowledge of your coming soon is sending strong vibes through my whole body intensifying my need for you. I did not know that it could be possible to feel such passion for you even before our meeting. What I am so sure of is that, our love is so sacred and it seems like this relationship was made in heaven. I love you so very much Edward so much that it's even surprising me. I just feel it right inside and I am so convinced that we were meant for each other. There should be no question about that my darling. We just belong together. We belong to each other my love. Yes honey, I will wait for you until you come to me.

I will forever cherish the first time that I am going to see you. I just don't know what to do with myself. Can you imagine darling, its already after 11pm, so I will make sure that I will listen to your interview on radio. Darling I hope you have managed to write your article? How did your TV interview go?

I just feel that as soon as you finish your tight schedule, you should just come over here for some relaxation. You deserve a break from your hectic life style my darling. You need to slow down, even for health reasons.

After finishing writing this mail, I will have to listen to some of the music you forwarded to me love whilst waiting for the midnight hour so as to listen to your interview on radio. I love you Edward, honest I do.

Darling tomorrow it would be only 14 days to go. I love you darling Edward. I will be waiting for you honey. Indeed you are the best thing in my life.

I LOVE YOU,
Melody.

#46 Ed responds to challenges but is convinced everything will be fine

July 15, 2010

Dear Melody,

Good Morning Sunshine!

I tried to send you an early morning greeting with a photo I took today at lunch but it seems that the flash did not go off due to the fault of the waitress. Anyhow I am sending it regardless.

Hope you had a great night's sleep, especially that you were tired. Yes - Good morning sunshine. I wish you a great day! Wow! 15 days to go. Am I right? I am now leaving on the 29th. That is what my Agent says. She called me frantically and said she had a great fare to Dar es Salaam. I suspect that the agents are getting problems with the Arusha leg so let me leave it in your hands so that we will be able to guarantee that you meet me on arrival. Thank you in advance. I will not like to arrive in Dar es Salaam and you are not on hand to reach me. I will be lost.

No one turned up for the case in court today. I had a bad day until you called. Darling it is wonderful; you reached me at my lowest moment. Thank you for lifting me up. I love you babes!

My assistant has accepted the position and we met with two referral agents and that meeting went well. I took the team, except my assistant to lunch and I met my favourite chef who joined us as his restaurant was closed. I had a few rum and coke and left the restaurant mellow and came home. I was on the computer as I had work to do and couldn't take a rest. I will be tired enough to sleep well tonight.

Thank you for the information you provided regarding medical facilities. It is said if you ask the cost, you can't afford. I will find out when I visit the massage therapist. She/he will be my first stop and I hope she/he would be great so I will be moved to give a tip as well.

Darling there is so much excitement. I just can't wait to be by your side. This is like dreaming but it is real. I have to pinch myself. I can't believe it and everything is moving fine even when things are not clear.

My exit is coming at a very hectic period. I told you about my itinerary last evening. Everything will be fine I will do my best not to do too much drinking.

Be good honey - have a great day. Remember love always finds a way. I love you honey. You mean everything to me.

Love always - Ed

#47 Melody takes note that excitement is building up

July 15, 2010

Edward my love,

Good morning, actually it's afternoon here. I suppose I have calmed down a bit now. I know it's real and I am still too happy but I think I am now managing to take stock of my emotions. WOW!!!! That is good news. Did I make sense in my previous mail? I think I should go back to it and read it again.

Well good morning darling. How are you today? Are you happy like me? Oh, God's life is just good. I don't know where to start. First and foremost, be assured of the fact that, I will be there in Dar es Salaam waiting for you on the 29th. No matter what, I will be there, come rain, come sunshine; I will be waiting for you. I LOVE YOU so very much. Nothing, I repeat, nothing can stop me from being there for you, for us.

Secondly, I am just waiting for the itinerary so that I do all the bookings. There is no problem there at all. About the massage therapist, well, I might have, to have a go at you first before we think of taking you to whichever parlour for a massage. Ever heard of that darling? What do you say to that? Yes, I will massage you first and foremost, then perhaps if you still think it would be necessary, you can visit the parlours. I think I can do most of what is done there if not more. It's so funny, right? Well we will see what's best for both of us. I am laughing while writing this. I am sure you will be saying, "What on earth is this?" Never mind, if you discover that I am still an amateur in that field, then I can just as well practice on you. I love you Ed.

I saw the picture. It's not very clear, alright but I will see if I can work on it a bit to make it light so as to see you more clearly. Thank you for sending it anyway. I believe that, what counts more is the thought. So thank you my love. If I manage to improve it, then I will let you know. If I fail, who knows you might send me another one in its place. I am addicted to your pictures.

So your assistant agreed to the new terms of engagement? That is good. I am happy for her. At least she is not completely without a job.

Do you want to know where there is too much excitement? It is here darling. This morning I nearly failed to contain myself. Want to know something. I only managed to see your love note with this coming home information much later. I just don't know how I could not have seen it earlier.

I had then assumed that since you were too busy, maybe you had failed to write my morning love note. However, I was just happy that you had at least written something. Oh Edward, this is the best news I have heard in a very long time. I feel in love and loved more than anyone in the world. I just want you to know beyond any reasonable doubt that this girl loves you like no one else has ever loved you. That is the truth. Yes, I love you Edward, I really do.

So its 15 days left? Hooray! I am beside myself with ecstasy. My happiness can reach everywhere in the world and beyond. Just to be close to you Ed, you mean the world to me.

Is this love that I am feeling? Edward, like one Reggae artist sang, "I wanna love you, every day and every night". That is the truth. Ed I want to love you, kiss and hug you, everyday. Our togetherness, to me will be like heaven. I am really looking forward to your arrival with MY EVERYTHING. It is a good thing that the young lady from the travel agency is going to reserve your seat. I can just say that she is God sent.

So how are you feeling about the whole thing my love? Are you as excited as I am? Well since I am still at work, I will write you a proper letter when I am about to go to bed.

Thank you very much for this piece if information. It has brought me back to life my love. At least now we can count only up to fifteen. I love you Eddie.

Enjoy the rest of your afternoon and God will bless you even more for both our sakes.

You have to take care of yourself. I have asked God to do that as well for me, since you are all what I have. Ed, you are the best thing that ever happened to me.

Melody

#48 Ed requests that Melody gives leadership with love

July 16, 2010

Dear Melody,

Happy Saturday! This is a hectic weekend in St. Lucia. People get back to work in earnest on Wednesday. You are so wonderful! I love you. I am getting a host of pictures for you from last night and tonight and right through the weekend you going to get plenty of pictures of the Indian wedding, etc.

Darling, I am having the time of my life. We must have some of these days and nights when I get there. We will go crazy in Dar es Salaam. It will be unfair for me not to give you some Caribbean excitement. I used to dance very well at one time. I think I still remember to do a thing or two on the floor. I won a prize for Limbo dancing in Trinidad a few years ago.

Just for you, I gave thought to the fact that I will have to balance our agenda. I hope you love that. That is how considerate I am. I think about me but I think a lot about you. So you know what, our first few weeks, we will let our hair down and decide what adjustments we should make along the way. Is that fair? Is that the way you would rather it be???? It's not me, it is us. I told you once or maybe a few times, I will want you to be the one in charge. I repeat, please don't take advantage of me. Although I think your love for me will never allow you to do such a thing as taking advantage of me.

Let us keep our love on fire and nothing will go wrong. I love you honey. You mean a lot to me. Enjoy Saturday. Have a restful weekend. Just one more weekend and I will be getting really close to my being in Arusha. Thirteen Days to go. I can't believe it.

I am rushing off to the meeting.

Love Always – Eddie

#49 Melody promises to be considerate in her leadership role

July 17, 2010

Darling Edward,

Good Afternoon.

Talking to you always gives me a new lease of life. YOU, BEING IN MY LIFE GIVES ME A PROPER SENSE OF PURPOSE. Edward, you are my TOMORROW. You are the best thing that ever happened to me. This kind of love you have made me aware of in me is something so good and new to me. I just don't think I can ever be able to live without you in my life. You must be the whole purpose for me to have been put in this world. Edward you are my love and my life.

Thank you my darling for your love note and for your being so considerate of my feelings too. You seem to have the qualities that I yearn for in my man. I think I understand you. So when you are here, we will plan together, change anything as we see fit. That makes sense.

When in Arusha, we will be going to some nice and interesting places. We can even go to some very interesting night spots. I somehow feel that we can have fun anywhere, as long as we are together.

Darling I wish that you enjoy yourself at the wedding in the South. I have seen all the pictures you have sent. Thank you. It looks like you were really busy. You are looking so good darling. You really outshine them all.

Thank you darling. Are you even aware that you are a natural star? Edward you are my hero. Darling I know that our love is so pure, so real and so strong that nothing can take it from us. I will never take advantage of you in any way for it would be like doing that to me. I feel like we are one already darling. Injuring you in any way is just like doing it to me. I feel we are already one, and are united in love. Edward, I mean it when I say that I love you. It's like you are the best part of me darling. So rest assured that nothing bad will come from me, for you are my all. I love you the way I love myself. So please remember that always.

Ed, you are the most important thing in my life. I am so comforted that you are coming. I cannot wait my love. Please, take care darling, you are all that I have.

Love,
Melody

#50 Edward points to the future with Melody

July 18, 2010
Dear Melody,
Hello Darling, Happy Sunday!!

It is a wonderful evening and the day was very hectic. Met old friends, had some Indian food. I drank only one beer. I disciplined myself so that I will live to fight another day. Tomorrow is another day and the fun begins at 5.00pm. I plan to spend no more than 4 hours and drive back down to Castries as on Monday I would like to get some cleaning up done and move furniture from my old office.

Nothing will be happening in St. Lucia until Wednesday of next week. So it is going to be a short week. Closure will be made on a few matters and as I promised the next time we talk about my trip, will be when you see my confirmed itinerary. Baby, are you ready for me? Are you ready to put your hand in my hand as together we will navigate a new chapter in our lives? I love you Melody, you mean everything to me. Our future together is in the hands of God. Only He can make our dreams reality.

So you enjoyed the photos? It was interesting that your remarks about my coordination repeated later in the evening by a few young ladies who gathered for the social get together after the meeting at the hotel. I love to dress up. My mother taught me to look my best.

I will be taking some carnival shots for you. It is going to be crazy in the streets Monday and Tuesday. You have turned me into a photographer, anything for your love baby.

Only twelve days to go. It is getting closer and closer. I can't believe it's all coming together now, and soon we will be together. How is my baby daughter? Have a blessed Sunday. I love you.

Love always - Ed

#51 Melody is addicted to Ed's love notes
July 18, 2010
Darling,

What I know for sure is that you are all that I need. I can give up anything for you. I can't even understand it myself. How can this be possible? How come I am so lost to you? How could a total, complete stranger, manage to have such a strong impact on me? It's only God who can answer that I suppose. Ed, you have won me. You can rest assured that I have surrendered my whole being into your hands. You can do whatever you want with me, I am all yours.

Actually, it's me who should be worried about being taken advantage of. Oh man, this feeling is so strong, strange and very real. I LOVE YOU and that is that. I love to know that you also seem to be feeling the same. Ed we can start our life together. I see that being just natural and the truth.

Don't worry, the pictures can come later. Thank you for the morning love note. I am more addicted to it than you can believe. You seem to be my reason to wake up every morning. I am so addicted to your love. Let's hope I won't be overcome with emotion in Dar es Salaam. You are now my reason that I want to be alive. I am living for you Edward.

I will keep on loving you. I will cherish you forever darling no matter what might happen. Just know that you are the centre of my life. I will give my all to this relationship. I will give you all of me. I love you Ed. I am looking forward to your coming with every fibre in me. You are my man. You are my all. You answer for all what I need in a man. I love you. I need and miss you.

Ed, I hope to talk with you on the phone during the day. Take care, for you are the most precious thing I have. You are my treasure darling.

I love you,
Melody.

#52 Melody reveals all the reasons for loving Ed
July 19, 2010
Edward,

Thank you my love for making the call. I was feeling so empty without having seen your love note. Although I knew very well that you were at the wedding and could have stayed until early morning hours, still my heart was yearning for your love note all the same.

Should we call it some addiction of some kind? Darling it's apparent that I am hooked on your love. I have become a part of you. I just can't do without your sweet loving. So when you called, you made my day. Thank you my darling. I love you so very much. Last night was phenomenal. The fact that I could see you live on Skype made me realize beyond any doubt that you are all that I need. You are just my type, my size and my all. You asked whether you looked to me, as a stern teacher. You just looked like a lover and you also looked to be on the stubborn side. You know a person who means what he says and who wants to see what he anticipates. You look like someone who knows what they want and who can insist to see the result of whatever they are looking forward to. You seem to carry this unwavering spirit within you. You look like a born optimist and a natural achiever. You look like your attitude towards life is that of a person who is assured of how things are going to turn out like before even any result comes out. You have this look that can subdue a woman if you really want to. I literally melted with love just by looking at you. I was trying hard to keep my emotions under control since our children were around. It was such a struggle for me. It was also so funny. I just discovered one truth Edward, that I love you with all my heart. You were even from a distance, managing to affect every emotion in me. Where did you come from Edward Harris and where have you been all along?

Surely you are my mystery or should I rather just call you my miracle? You are just my unexpected good fortune, my wonder and my blessing. I love you Edward. I was just wondering whether the passion you portray even when you are just looking at someone would remain there for all the days we would be together. I also wondered how you would look, when you are not happy with something or someone.

In your presence, I just knew that I would just tremble due to your nearness and the love I was likely to feel. Oh God, I felt all my weakness towards you. I felt so feminine and helpless by just looking at you. I tried to cover all those mixed feelings by smiling. I think I tried to keep my composure in front of the children. My daughter was watching me and later she told me that it was the first time she saw me in love with anyone. She said that all along she thought I was not sexual in any way. She said she just saw my relationship with her father as one void of passion or sexuality. She just saw us as good as a brother and sister who were so close. She told me that she had never imagined that we ever made love at all. That was so unbelievable coming from her. I asked her how on earth she thought they came into the world. She went on to say she knew how children came about but it was so difficult for her to imagine that her father and me were ever in a sexual relationship or in a whirlwind of love as the love she has seen in my life from the time I started having a relationship with you. She said she was happy that I was so happy, alive and in love in such a way. It's just unbelievable to hear my daughter say that about me. I know I am in love with you alright but I never thought that the child could be able to observe the difference. Isn't that amazing? However, I told her that it is true that I am in love and that I pray to God that it remains that way. I told her that it was indeed a wonderful and rare feeling.

Edward, so how are you darling? I know you must be sleeping now. I always wish if you could be sleeping beside me. Oh, did I tell you that I love your arms? I can imagine your embrace and your touch to be out of this world. Is it me or is it you triggering these feelings, especially in me? Ed, you are so different from everyone I met. I just feel so close to you. I feel so much in love with you in a way that sometimes frightens me.

This morning I managed to have my daughter shoot some photos of me. I was failing to smile somehow. I was missing you so very much. So enjoy seeing how miserable I can be when I miss you. I have also attached some shots that were taken out by my son while he was on holiday.

Are you awake now darling? So you will be driving home sometime today isn't it? Days are moving and I am full of anticipation since you will be coming. It's already afternoon here. The morning was busy. In the afternoon I will be in the cyberspace with users, at the reference desk.

I am thinking of you. In you darling, I have found all what I EVER needed in a man. I love the way you look. I love your maturity. I love your playfulness. I adore your laughter. I love your attitude towards life. I like how positive you are about life. I love you for your courage, your guts and the way you trust and love me. I will forever appreciate and cherish the way you love me. I like the way you write. Edward I love you for a hundred thousand reasons, but most of all I love you because you are YOU.

Darling welcome, to a brand new day. I wish that all your heart's desires will materialize. Good morning Edward. Good morning my all. Thank you for being there for me. I will love you forever.

Melody

#53 Melody seeks assurance that Ed will be everything to her

July 19, 2010

HEYA!!!

Thank you for the second call. You have indeed blessed my day twice already. I want to tell you that I did not revise your love note. I love the way your voice sounds when you are just waking up. You sound as if you will be in the mood for love. Am I wrong? So in turn you put me in the mood for you. Can you believe that?

Edward, how I wish you to be the first thing I see every day when I wake up!!!

I also wish that you will be the last thing I see all my days before I fall asleep. Yesterday on Skype you had this playfulness look in your eyes and I felt like I could just run into your arms and melt with desire. You really know how to tease my feelings naturally. I love you for that Ed. I know beyond doubt that God had me in mind when he made you. Oh God, this is real and good and lovely. You make me so happy.

When you called the first time you sounded tired and sleepy, romantic and so good, or should I say you had the sexiest voice I have ever heard? I love the way you sound. When you are excited you have a different voice. You sound happy, alert, very much in tune with me. When you are tired you sound so much in love, serious and ready to love me to bits. When sleepy, you somehow sound as if you would never want me to leave your side, like you would like me to hold onto you until eternity. You sounded as if you just want to see ONLY me in this wide and wonderful world. You sounded as if you were just yearning for me and as if you could have kissed me until I would be so breathless and ready to cry out because of loving you too much. Edward, I love you. You can at least see a bit of how my imagination runs away with me. Is this love that I am feeling darling? Do you ever feel for me? Ever imagine me in any way? Ever imagine me going crazy for you? I LOVE YOU MY EDWARD. WELL LET ME ATTEND TO SOMETHING HERE. I FEEL LIKE KEEPING ON WRITING TO YOU MY LOVE. Today, I am on fire for you. Have you seen the pictures I sent you? Any comment? I am tempted to have one taken now so that you see what the office can do to me. At least I am so happy since we have talked.

Edward, can you see that you have become the pivot of my life? Tell me what am I going to do with such feelings? Are you sure you will stand by me all the time, through rain, sunshine and through it all? Will you keep on loving me in spite of whatever darling? You are all that I need in my life. You're the answer to my every feminine need, whim, fantasy and fetish. I am in love with you Edward.

Melody

#54 Ed introduces Melody to St. Lucia's Carnival
July 20, 2010
Dear Melody,
Good Morning Darling!

I have been over doing it; I have to stop especially the late nights. I stopped drinking for 5 years, 2 years, so sometimes I tell myself enough is enough so I think I am at that stage now.

I am back on my feet again, haven't left home since I arrived. It is time to rest so that I can get a few things done when I wake up in the morning.

I am glad that you like the pictures. You don't need another picture of me until you see me in person. Your pictures were great. You look as you are an international woman. I guess you create a stir in the office. I like your boots. I am always happy to see a photograph of you. I love you babes. I look forward with all my being to be close to you.

Your letters today were wonderful. It was great that we could have met over cyberspace yesterday. It was a pleasure. It seemed as though we were next to each other. Technology can really make a difference in the way we communicate today.

Tomorrow is a half day holiday so the town will be locked down at noon. Carnival is when the women show off everything. There is nothing left to the imagination. You can check it out live at www. choice39.tv Then, I don't have to send you photographs. If you check and the station is off be sure to check back. You are going to love it. If you go on line and they are not streaming, please check back. 1.00pm should be ideal but they might be streaming Monday's highlights.

I am trying to write but I am not with it. I am going to be very busy tomorrow. I will be going into the city and checking with the printer to get my Home Coming Fair advertising. There is never a dull moment. It is all as quoted in my headline for last weekend.

Words fail me. I am hoping that even when I am speechless you will love me. So today, we had a lot to sustain us, telephone call, photo exchange and love notes.

Stay in your section is the hit calypso/song this year.

Love you – Ed

#55 Melody challenges Edward to be responsive to her love

July 20, 2010

Darling Ed,

Welcome back to the land of the living darling. I know it's not funny, but it can be amusing when it's over. If you managed at one time to refrain from alcohol for a stretch of 5 years or even 2 years it means that you can stop whenever you decide. I just love you even when drunk, with a hangover, when still recovering from one, or even after having recovered from one. I just love you Edward.

So tell me how do you feel now? Get back, recover fast from the hangover for you have a lot to do. This week is one of your busiest weeks I take it. You have to be as fit as a fiddle before you travel darling. Someone is dying to be with you. You have to be on top of things. So get well soon my love.

So you also like my picture? Darling I have this feeling or conviction that we are meant for each other. We deserve each other and we were tailor -made to suit. I love you with such a passion that you will never know. I need you darling and you are constantly on my mind.

Darling you were still too tired to write a long note. I could tell, but still I could feel you more. The little that you wrote meant volumes to me. I could sense the sentiments imbedded in your every word. It looked like each and every word was impregnated with a hidden meaning, spelling and portraying all the notes so easy to express the true love feelings you have for me. Could I be imagining things darling? No, for the way I feel your feelings even the unexpressed feelings is so real to me.

I seem to sense volumes of your heart's innermost feelings for me. My heart seems to be communicating with your heart in a hidden language of love. Does this make sense to you Edward? Could it be telepathy? Is this realistic in this life? Why is it that my heart, soul and spirit seem to be in rhythm with yours, yet you are so far away? I seem to understand you not with my head but with my heart and my feelings. Oh Edward I am just lost in you. Will you please try to find me for me? I am lost in your love. I am completely immersed, gone into you.

Edward please get this straight, I have never loved anyone like this. I want our love to be successful. I want to be all what you might ever need. I want us to start all over and do the best job of this love thing again and in the best possible way. I want us to be exemplary in this world. I want to rely on you in everything. I would want us to do justice to this love that we claim we feel for each other.

I will love you to bits, or maybe I should say my love will take us to some new heights that we would have never thought possible. I want to love you, kiss and hug you every day. You seem to be the best thing in my life Ed. Please come and fly with me in this strange feeling. Come let's disappear into oblivion. Come let's live in this Utopia I have discovered called love. It's possible yes. Yes, I believe in us and most of all I believe in YOU.

Darling I am ready for you. I am ready for your love. I am ready for any possible commitment to you. I am ready to run this race with you. I don't care how it might sound or look like to this world. All I know is that the two of us can do this. We can manage this. We can survive whatever this life can bring to us. Actually, we will do very well together. We will be more than fine. We can overcome anything in our path. Yes, we can overcome any adversity.

Look darling my heart is already conquered by your love. I can do anything for this love of ours. I am prepared and ready, actually I feel that I am all yours. So Darling Edward, we have to do the best for ourselves. I love you and I am convinced that you do the same. Together, we will be so happy and so compatible. We will teach each other on the way. You will do most of the teaching and instructing and coaching on whatever I need to learn, know or master. Then we will trust God with all else and God will do the rest for us.

Welcome to my world of fantasy darling. Now I can't do without you in my life. Do you regret having met me so far?

Continued/

Edward, good morning my love! Do you feel how I love you? Now it looks like I am placing a huge responsibility on your shoulders, the responsibility of nurturing my love, the responsibility of loving me back. The knowledge that you are loved beyond reason or measure, the realization that someone is madly in love with you and can't let go of you. Darling I am hooked on you, so tell me what should I do? Still want to put up with such madness? Are you brave enough for such a kind of loving Edward? Will you cope with me honey? Are you prepared to be tied down to a new life with me?

I am glad you also love my picture darling. I am glad to note that you find me attractive and are attracted to me honey as I am attracted to you. I just don't know Edward. All I know is that I am madly in love. I hope and trust that you will love me back. I will love you with all my heart and more.

This is something so new to us I suppose, this kind of loving. All the same, I trust God and our feelings that it will be there forever. Take me if you want me Edward. Love me if you will for you have won control of me.

Good morning my love. How do you feel this morning?
Melody.

#56 Ed has a vision of Financial and Time Freedom
July 21, 2010
Dear Melody,
Good Morning my Love!

Hope you had a restful night in spite it appears as though you went to bed late. I am hoping that you awake with the necessary energy to see you through the day. Remember I love you honey and very soon our desires will be fulfilled. It was God's will that we met and it will be his will to see us through. Let us affirm that we will be together as planned.

Everything will be OK! The way we feel for each other must be manifested in reality. Our burning desire for our coming together has already been realized in heaven and it is said in the good book what is bound on earth is bound in heaven. The Secret declares that our faith is built on three action principles - Believe - Ask - Receive! We have done everything to make it possible for us to reap the fruits of our labour.

Do you believe I didn't leave home today as indicated when we spoke and I am glad I didn't plan to as the rain fell for most of the afternoon. It was a rain soaked Carnival. I watched on the TV. I didn't miss anything. My friend called me to join him but I said I will pass. I am getting away from strong drink. I feel I had enough for the past few days. I have to exercise control. Tomorrow is a hectic day so I must be ready.

God will forever grant us the desires of our hearts, especially when they are in His will. Our love is bonded together and it is our prayer that it will last forever. Melody, I love you with every breath I breathe. You are always on my mind. I keep making the point that I want to make a new start and I am putting my best efforts to realize our dreams. When you write to me I feel your heart beat, when you speak with me I am breathlessly kissed. Something special is happening in our lives. As I write to you I am mostly smiling as our conversation seems as though we are next to each other. When I write to you I feel no distance between us. I feel you next to me.

I have begun to speak about our first anniversary. That first milestone will be our reference point. As our love and appreciation for each other has grown over the months, it is my sincere wish that our love will prosper with every passing day and we will get closer to each other, feeling each other's heartbeat even when we are not having an embrace with our arms around each other. I feel like flying into your arms. I can't wait any longer. It is very painful to live this experience but it is this experience that has moulded us and will further cement our love when we get together to enjoy all the things we now wish for.

The future seems so exciting that we will have to manage our time and never attempt to move the process faster than we should, if we are to maintain our programme of leisure. What did I promise - when you arrive home I will be waiting for you and devote my evenings to you only. We will chat about our day but never work on projects. Let us see how that will work because there is so much excitement about our projects.

How many weeks holiday per annum are you entitled to? We can go away not necessarily out of Tanzania whenever we need to brain storm. We will live the life we love. My goal is to live a life of Financial and Time Freedom, even earning money even when I am sleeping.

Have a blessed day and as always, remember someone loves you honey!

Love always - Ed

#57 Melody vents her frustrations regarding the long wait

July 21, 2010

Darling Ed,

You should be still asleep at this moment. I could have enjoyed just watching you sleeping and let my heart melt with loving and adoring you. I could have pecked you on the lips and smiled at you. My heart would then tell God that it loves the man sleeping and prayed that God keep him protected. You might never realize how much you are loved by me. I know we will be together soon and that's very comforting.

Thank you for your note of this morning. It has showered, and enveloped me with love and filled me up with reassurance. You can even manage to pamper me with love from that far. It just amazes me. I didn't know how vulnerable I become when I have not received your love note. It's just so frightening. I am now relying on you in so many ways that I never thought would be practical.

Your telephone calls actually brought out to me what kind of person you are. Ed, you are a wonderful person with the perfect attitude like I have never seen before. You make me feel like a woman in every respect. You are turning me into a proper woman. I love you more for it. I just love all what you believe in and stand for. I like the way you take life. You stand for all what I take as a real, perfect and undiluted man. I just love you with all the passion that my body and mind can muster. You mean the world to me.

I understand what you meant by that you can't leave someone to finalize business deals/transactions for you. I know that it's true, that it's not easy with money. You know darling, what I am concerned about mostly is that we have at least to get together soon and do all the catching up that we have to do in person, even if that might mean you will still have to go back for a while to finalize all the outstanding business deals in St Lucia. Only knowing that you would be coming back to Arusha after tying up all the business loose ends would be fine with me.

What's killing me is this waiting whilst burning and yearning for your love. It's just such punishment since the time I got to know you, it seems like it has become so difficult to be on my own. I know we are doing the best in the situation. I also like the principle of Believe - Ask - Receive!

I believe in that and with you I agree to that. Darling the best thing that has happened so far is that of discovering each other. That miracle could not have been easy to realize without God himself. The rest about business is just fine, it can be resolved without much problems.

So you did not go out? That was a wise choice on our part since you need the body to recover and get all the energies that it will need for all that which is lined up for you to do.

Thinking of our first anniversary? That has made me believe more in us. Making a new start, Wow Ed, you are all what I need in this new life. You make this such a reality darling.

I love your love note. Ed we will surely make it together lets dream big. I am with you all the way. I trust that with you in this dream life, all things are possible. I believe in us and more in you darling.

I feel and know it beyond doubt that you belong with me. My arms are yearning to hold you. I am dying to tell you personally that we belong together. We will make a new start and see to it that it works. The fact that we love each other is the most crucial and most important step in our relationship.

Alright I will watch the websites those links you have provided. It always pays to be at the right place at the right time. You never cease to amaze me. Ed, you are just my miracle, that's all I can say and I praise God for your coming into my life darling. All I know is, if it's me writing about how I feel for you, that I can do tirelessly. It seems like the only subject I have confidence to write about is YOU. All I feel about you, all my thoughts about you, all my imaginations about you. Ask me for that, I can write with such ease. Otherwise, the rest, you will have to make my brain think. You have to train my brain on anything else.

I just love the way you write about us, the way you express our love for each other and the way you talk so well about what our loving each other entails. You also just convince my feelings and all, when you talk about our future and what it holds in store for us. Darling you are the most level headed man I have ever come across. You are the best planner that I have ever seen. Oh God how you convince me darling and the faith you give me, I believe in your every word and believe in all that you are capable of becoming. You just bring me to life even if I might have been feeling blue. You just pull me out of any possible depression. I love you my darling Edward. You just know how to drive me crazy with love for you. You know how to put purpose into my life. You are good at colouring beautiful rainbows into my once plain life. You turn me alive with love and anticipation. Please darling, never think of ever leaving me. I am so addicted to you and your loving. I don't think I can ever manage to carry on alone in this life without you. I need you in my life forever Edward.

Darling I love the way you love me. I love you taking your place in my heart. You are my man, I am your woman. I feel that is the way it should be from now onwards.

Good morning dearest Edward. Welcome to a brand new day with all the challenges it holds. I wish for you to subdue all the challenges that might come your way. Yes, with God on your side you will overcome.

I will write later my darling. I love you with everlasting love.
Melody

#58 Melody stresses that love will conquer all
July 21, 2010
Darling Edward,

Thanks for this note. I know what that long list of medical requirements can imply in one's mind. We felt the same way when we came to Arusha the first time. Yes, you can get all the other vaccines here, no big deal. I have had lots of people come to visit from home, having been vaccinated for yellow fever only. That is the one they are mainly concerned about, so you will be fine.

I got your call. Thanks for calling. I heard all what you said and am not discouraged. These things can happen but we will be fine one way or the other. This can't change us or our feelings towards each other in any way. Listen darling, I still love you if not even more than before.

Like you said, all things work together for good to us ward who love Christ and who are made according to His purpose. We will overcome this. As a rule, we have to be thankful for everything. The best news is, we are in love and everything is going to turn out fine. Whatever it takes, I will wait for your arrival in Dar es Salaam. Whether it could be on the 31st of July or the 31st of August, I will practice some patience my love. Nothing will ever get between us, that's a promise. Nothing will take my loving you from me either, no darling for that will never be. I will wait no matter how long it takes.

It's home time now, so I will be writing you from home later. Let me go and see how my baby and the maids are doing since my daughter is away. Everything will turn out fine that I know beyond any doubt. We will be fine sooner rather than later. I will be in touch with you from home. I LOVE YOU EDWARD TILL THE END OF TIME. Take good cheer darling. We are still alive and in love. Love is a gift that supersedes all other things. Oh by the way, I have taken photos for you today so that you can see how I was looking today in the office. You are the love of my life Edward.

Melody

#59 Melody is determined to overcome all obstacles
July 22, 2010
My darling Edward,

I have been listening to music all along and just thinking of us. Darling are you aware that we are so blessed that we found each other in the first place? I have come to the realization of how lucky we are to be having what we have? You know what Edward, I could just as well have opted for our love instead of many life treasures or pleasures if we could have been asked to chose.

If we were given a choice between what we could have been anticipating in terms of money or whatever, I would still have chosen you. I would have chosen our love. Our getting together will happen one way or the other. Being together is just going to happen no matter what it takes. The fact that we have the love we have is such a treasure which I am beginning to see in its entirety.

I thank God for having given me you. I will forever be grateful to God who made it possible for us to discover each other and gave us the capability to love each other with such a rare passion that many people don't ever experience here on earth. I just thought I should write this so as to bring this to your attention as well. I LOVE YOU MY DARLING EDWARD

SO, HOW HAS BEEN YOU DAY SO FAR? I will be sleeping soon. We have every reason to smile and be thankful you see. You are all what I need and a lot more. You are my jewel and my treasure. You are my Knight in shining armour Edward. You should keep positive and believe that everything else will soon fall into place. That fact that we have each other and are so much in love is enough reason to make me happy. Coming here, of course you will eventually do, we have no choice since I strongly feel that we are destined to spend the rest of our lives together. The way we came to be in each other's lives is truly amazing and unbelievable. That same force, which propelled us to get to be together with such intense passion, will also see us through. Whatever obstacles that we may encounter on our way to our intended destination - staying together, will soon be behind us.

You are the love of my life, no matter what it takes, we will be together soon.

Melody

#60 Ed expresses confidence that Love will find a way

July 22, 2010

Dear Melody,

Happy Day!

I want you to know that you are my special angel sent from heaven above. Nothing will put us off course. I love you and you love me. God has brought us together and nothing can come between us and prevent our coming together to happen.

My arrival will only be postponed for a few days, not weeks, not months. It is just that nothing is happening here to fast track my business. I will share with you an email from my friend in Canada who is selling the properties. It is so frustrating but it will all be concluded next week. All of the purchasers are too advanced to turn back. They are like us. We are too big to fail. Just keep the faith. Don't be afraid, everything will be OK I promise you or should I say we promised ourselves that nothing will change our love for each other.

When I come, I don't want to return, I will be burning my boat, I still feel the same as when we met on line. I want to be with you as much as you want to be with me. We shall have the desires of our hearts. I want to put my delay in arriving behind us. We must move on even with greater resolve. I keep praying that everything will be alright and we will definitely embrace each other and agree that reality has arrived - we are together at last.

Thank you for the information you provided regarding the vaccination issues. I will get whatever is necessary when I arrive and get the opportunity to check with the doctor. God will protect as He has always done. I visited the Fair pavilion today and was surprised that I still got the same booth. Did you check the website to see my listing?

Have a wonderful day. Don't worry, be happy. Remember Eddie loves you honey.

Be good.

Love always – Ed

#61 Ed is keeping the faith and trusting his Source to deliver

July 23, 2010

Dear Melody,

Good Morning Sunshine!

I enjoy the video you sent me but before I realized that it was a slide show, I had listened to the background music and sang along to the hymn - How great thou art??? God is great!!! We love him. He is a miracle worker.

You are a precious gift given to me by God. He fashioned you to meet the desires of my heart. I love you. I hope you had a good day and a peaceful night. May your day be filled with pleasant surprises as I keep you ever present in my thoughts. I love you! I am thrilled at the events of today. He will make a way when all seem impossible to us. I love Yahweh! He delivers every time and on time.

You were up very late. Just about when I was giving up on you, the email popped up. You always ensure that I get my love note before you retire. How can I not love you with all my heart? I want to be writing to you when you are sleeping. Well, the day has ended here and its twilight time. I am home. I went to the office and unfortunately the ICT technician did not turn up. He promised 11.00 am tomorrow. That is keeping me back I can't afford any set back in my time management.

Everything is going just fine with my clients and we are all looking forward to the finalization of business deals early next week. My plans for the Fair are progressing nicely and again everything is falling into place. You will definitely get pictures of the booth. I hope my printer does a good job of the banners. I will be having a raffle. Everyone visiting the booth will be given a chance to enter the raffle by placing their business card in the jar. At the end of the Fair the lucky winner's business card will be drawn.

You are very much the reason for what will happen in my life from here on. You made me fast track my dreams which will soon be reality.

As I indicated earlier today, I guess you are missing your daughter very much. Baby is holding the fort anyhow, so live with what you have until your life returns to normalcy. We now have only 7 days to our original itinerary. Baby it wouldn't be long. Have faith in the one you love and I will deliver on my promise. I know it will be possible and it will.

Be good and have a blessed day.

Love Always - Ed

#62 Melody expresses her deepest feelings for Ed

July 23, 2010

Edward,

I have been home for some time now. I have been reading your mail and looking at your pictures. I love you darling.

Baby keeps on saying baba is home whenever she sees your picture. She can pick you out even from all others in the picture. I love you my Edward. I think it's me who can't get enough of you and your loving. You have to excuse the way I write sometimes. When writing to you, sometimes I just put all my thoughts in their crude state into words. I seem to just write, no synthesizing anything.

Well, I am so happy that you like the pictures of today. What did your friend say about me? It's always interesting to hear people's comments about oneself. Want to know what a friend from work said to me? Well I showed her your picture, the one taken at the wedding and she went, "Oh God Melody this man is good, you are so lucky. Please give him even at least one child." I went oh dear God, what is wrong with us African women with wanting to have babies for our men!!! It can be a lot of fun how people react.

You know what Ed, in these parts of the world, if people hear that you have met your partner on the internet they either become concerned since most internet relations are not genuine. Well there is an element of truth, that we both know honey. The fact that this is Africa also, makes some people skeptical about internet love. So sometimes, I just tell some people what they want to hear. Stories like we had met once just for a brief moment when he came as a tourist or some such version. Well to my real friends and some people who have been exposed, I just spill the beans that I found my man on the internet. I just love you Ed. Even if I had met you in a bar, at a disco, at a holiday resort, on a plane or at a charity function, I would have still fallen in love with you. Ed darling, whether I could have met you in a dream I am sure I would have loved you just as well. That is the way I feel about you darling, for I am so much in love with you. I also realized that I keep on falling in love with you every day. Yes I keep falling and falling and falling, more in love with you darling. I am so much in love Edward.

When you mentioned only 7 days, I can't explain the joy I felt. I just don't know how to put it into words. Maybe during the night time when my emotions are high I might be able to explicitly describe what the realization of your coming does to me exactly. Edward, you are one in a million. Definitely, they can't be another you and will never be another you anywhere in this wonderful world of ours.

It's only you who makes me feel this way darling. When you arrive, this love will be cemented. I love you and all that comprises you honey. What I feel for you is so rare that I wonder how many people dead or alive have been given the opportunity by God to have an experience of such a love, and to feel loved like this. You just blow me away Edward. You are the one and only one who can make me feel this way. I thank God for you every single day.

DARLING I WANT YOU TO READ THIS AND KNOW HOW MUCH I NEED YOU.

I will keep on writing since this feeling inside me is keeping on persisting. Yes let's dream big and it will soon be reality, I can feel that in me and am more than convinced. I have faith in you my darling.

Eddie, I love you and I need you now. Edward, you are the best thing that ever happened to me. I don't want to imagine losing you for I know that my world would end. This kind of loving someone is very dangerous, but I can't help myself for this is what it has to be, I just can't help myself darling, for you have taken all my heart. I am all yours, to have and to hold. You are all that I will ever need, and that is just that.

Enjoy your day my darling, you are all that I need honey.

Melody

#63 Melody consoles Ed in the light of possible disappointment

July 26, 2010

Edward,

What I know beyond any doubt is that, God has a way of turning even hopeless situations around. Things will work out fine and soon too. God will respect your conviction that a man has to be a man and that is very biblical too.

Just let go and let God. He always surprises us every time darling. That is the way it is. We will be fine. You have done your part and God will do his work. Remember, when he gives, he does it abundantly, unto overflowing. He fills one's cup unto over flowing. That is how amazing God is. God remains God and He does not change. God always delivers darling.

I love you Edward. You are the love of my life.

Melody

#64 Ed confesses his faith

July 26, 2010

Dear Ms. ………….

Good Morning my Love!

Hope your night produced the results you anticipated, if nothing else, a peaceful period of sleep. I wish your day will be very productive and set the pace for the week ahead. This new week is so important to me I don't even want to think about it.

This has to be my fulfillment week so that I can fulfill my promise to you. I can't go on another week without concluding my businesses so I can get on the plane. It must happen. I am trusting for a break through. It has been weeks of going forward and backward, and it must be concluded without any further delay. I am not scared, there is too much at stake. I am looking forward for the best results this week. Nothing happens before its time for us believers. I am looking forward to being with you. Don't worry, be happy!

Maybe I will have two love notes for you before you awake. It is getting to me now and I must admit I am stumped. I don't want to think about what if. I am not seeing any further delay, let us be strong for each other, there is too much at stake and baby I have to do it my way. I am a serious gambler and a networker who leverages his connections at the right time. It is all about timing and striking the right note. I believe that a man is born to lead in a considerate manner and do what is expected of him. I will come out of this long struggle in my usual confident way. In the end, I will once again say it was good - God is Great! Alleluia!

Have a blessed week.

Love always - Ed

#65 Melody thanks God for Ed

July 26, 2010

Edward,

HELLO!!!

I am aware of the fact that you are busy but just want to check on you. How has been your day so far? You are always on my mind. I am home now, have been for the past 2 hours. My daughter has landed at Kilimanjaro Airport. I sent a driver to get her. Had to come home and cook and be with Baby. I always wish if you were home, here.

Well you will be here soon so there is no need to worry but to be happy instead. Thank you for the morning love notes. You know I thrive on them. Your love shapes my day for me. Your love is like the morning sun. It gives light to my life. You give me direction darling. You are my morning sun. Edward you brighten my thoughts for the day. You give me strength to face the day and you give me enough reason to be joyful. Your love notes give me the reason to be rejoicing throughout the day. You make me face the world with my head high and overcome any obstacles.

You are my reason to praise God. You have even enhanced my praying pattern. You have revived me to trust and thank God once more. Edward you have managed to change my backsliding and gave me once more awareness that God has not forsaken me but loves me with an everlasting love.

Edward you have been my guiding light back to God. You have given me a fresh awareness that God can restore and renew us in ways abundantly above what we can wish for. You have brought God's presence back into my once resentful life. Your love has given me a new way of thinking which has restored my prayerfulness.

I love you darling. You are like an angel sent to me for the purpose of restoring love, happiness, joy, faith and a lot more. Like I said in the morning brief love note, when God gives he gives more than what we would have anticipated. You, Edward were given to me by God in order to console me, love me, keep me company, and give me friendship, trust, hope and a renewed sense of well being.

You have managed to restore me back to normalcy. You are my answered prayer, a prayer, mostly expressed by tears and groaning. You are God's answer, a miraculous answer. You are my miracle. God gave me the best, YOU, a lot more than I could have imagined possible. He, God, gave me you who seem to carry all the attributes I ever wished for. It's not easy to find a package which is so sufficiently fashioned. In you, God well catered for me. He cares for me greatly. He honoured me and gave me my PRIDE, my HERO, My Prince Charming, My Destiny, My LOVE and a lot more. You are the answer for a lot in my life. Edward, can God really be so generous? I will forever be so grateful for such a gift. I will forever love, cherish, treasure and give you the best care I can muster. I LOVE YOU Ed. You are more than special. I am so proud to have you in my life.

At times I wish you knew how special and how tailor made you are to me, you give me every reason to be happy in this wonderful world. I will forever love you darling. Edward you were meant to be mine by God himself. God allowed our past lives to be what it was, not by accident, not at all, it was all meant for us to be able to be together with renewed strength in a manner pleasing to Him. I can now thank God for everything that was, and what is, and what will be. God is in control, in charge and all.

So Edward we have every reason to be together, we have every reason to rejoice and every reason to thank God and all the reasons to celebrate that we are in God's purpose. I love everything about you. I love even the flaws or weaknesses you might have, known and yet to be known. You are my portion from God. I am and will be contented by ONLY YOU. I JUST THOUGHT YOU NEED TO KNOW THIS, FOR THIS IS HOW I FEEL ABOUT THIS RELATIONSHIP AND HOW IT CAME TO BE.

We were designed and fashioned by God to meet and satisfy each other's needs and wants. We have come thus far and God will fulfill His purpose by bringing us together. I love you my Edward. I feel humbled by God's greatness.

Well darling, enjoy the rest of the day and later a peaceful and restful night. Always remember, I will forever be all yours, to have and to hold.

Melody

#66 Ed reports progress on all fronts

July 27, 2010
Dear Melody,
Good Morning!

Hope that your night was great! Sweet dreams and everything nice. The day has progressed very well on all fronts. There is hope, we can only be encouraged. We will watch the week unfold.

Your love lifts me higher. I am happy you read the story and liked the picture. Here are some photos of the opening ceremony of the fair and my booth. There is also a photograph of the young lady you spoke with in her booth. Hope you enjoy. It was refreshing to note that you like designing. I have an eye for great designs.

I am very encouraged that your faith in God has been restored. I will be happy even if that is the only good that comes out of our relationship but rest assured there will be many more successes for both of us to be proud about. I love you Melody and continue to pray that everything will work together for good. Thank you for your encouragement and support.

I am hoping that tomorrow will be a better day at the exhibition. It was very slow today. However, each day brings it own fortunes whether good or bad. I look forward to a better day.

When we spoke today you mentioned you were sending me some

pictures of yourself at work. You failed to deliver. However, I understand. You are really wonderful and because you are so beautiful I will always let you off the hook. You mean a lot to me. I will always love you. I hope you, wake up to the joys of life knowing that someone loves you honey!!!

Love always – Ed

#67 Melody loves her package

July 27, 2010

Darling Edward,

Good morning. I love you. I love the whole of you. I love everything to do with you. I like your article. I love your stubborn faith. I like the way you look honey. I love the way you are. Your big brown eyes are killing me with love. I am always imagining what those nice lips of yours can do to me. I love YOU Edward Harris.

I have seen you yes. I love what I see, and I see what I love. The whole package darling I will take with gratitude. I am taken, I have fallen. I am gullible to your love, hook, line and sinker.

Darling it's true this is a crucial week but let's just stand stubbornly on faith, affirming our life together and all that has to come to pass. Like I said before, I will be your follower darling. You lead. Wherever you go I will follow. Whichever way you take that's my way. Whatever you believe in, we are in this together. I love you Edward. I am now a part of you and I will love you till the day you say you don't need me. Oh, I hope that will never be for I am lost forever in your love.

I have been very busy with visitors seeking information. Since you are now in my life, with you in my mind constantly, I even enjoy the once boring tasks. I love you Edward, so much that sometimes it hurts, but, I have found the paradox that, "if I love until it hurts, then there is no hurt, but only more love".

I will write your love note soon. You mean everything to me Edward. Good morning my love.

Melody

#68 Melody paints a portrait of her love

July 27, 2010
Edward,

Good afternoon. I suppose you are at the fair now, I miss being at your side darling. How is your day? Well most times the first day of an exhibition is naturally slow and uneventful. It is usually as the days progress that things start moving at the expected speed. So take heart darling, things will get moving before you know it.

Tell me honey, how do you feel today? I mean your temperament, your feelings towards everything? So you will be going to a meeting later? That's rather too much for a single day honey. Well maybe a man has to do what is required of him sometimes. I know you will survive all the pressure somehow, though honestly it's a lot of work for you. However, darling, I know very well that you are doing what you are doing for both of us. I appreciate that a lot my love.

Edward - are you even aware of how interesting you can get to be? I like your style. Just consider how you went on to reply my love note in bold, after each paragraph of mine, yes, paragraph after paragraph. That's interesting. It just gave the notes some coherence which end up depicting how the people who wrote rhyme. Oh, God, I like the way you just choose to do things somehow. You spice up my life. You can be so dramatic my love. You can give more meaning to whatever you choose. You don't cease to surprise me and cheer me up. Thank you.

About your eyes, I somehow can't doubt that at all. I even think age has enhanced the effect somehow, so please try by all means to restrict looking at the fairer sex just in case you might send the wrong vibes, or the unintended messages or intentions. You told me that you are through with other women now? So then maybe you will keep those eyes away from the opposite sex for both our sakes. LOL! It's so funny though. You are making me laugh as I write this. Those eyes should be for me only I suppose, right? Those romantic gazes should be reserved for me only. Well, well, maybe let the women enjoy your romantic gaze for the last time for soon you will be with me here. I love you Edward. I love your bedroom eyes.

So men like a challenge? Really Edward! Thanks for that. You really amuse me darling. I like the way you make me feel. Well we will see what goes on when you are here. Are you aware that you for one, are a great challenge darling? I will elaborate when you are here in person. I am so proud to have you as my man. You just do me proud, yes you are my pride.

I really appreciate the fact that you tell me that I have won control of you. See what I meant in one of my previous mail of today? You just caress my womanhood when you, the LION, with all the strength you possess, physically, mentally, emotionally, socially, sexually and God knows in which other areas I am yet to explore when we finally get together. You tell me that I can control you? I like the sound of that. I can understand the meaning of such sweet surrender, which depicts the degree of love you have for me. I love you more for that. You - darling with all your intelligence and exposure you have had in love, and life in general, and the territories in life you have subdued and conquered, you choose willingly to come and join me in this journey of love and you want me to take control of my great Lion? I love that honey. Be my special guest. I will make it a point that enough love envelopes you, giving you all the warmth that you deserve. I will make sure that your whole being is cushioned with tender loving care. Your senses are satisfied with the tingling sensations of love which is right and true.

Darling Edward, your life deserves to be tantalized by real, true and ever present love. Darling come and I will lay you between my breasts and sing you an African lullaby only composed by a heart which is so true. My arms will forever be there for you to wrap you tenderly so that your heart will forget all the past hurts and let downs you might have endured at the hands of God knows who. Edward come and let us make our hearts beat next to each other in rhythm to our love. Come my love, my lion and tease me with all you have within and without. Edward, we will be together soon and fulfill our feelings for each other. I really, really, love you dear man. I accept to take care and control of your loving heart. I am all yours and I accept all of you.

Enjoy the remainder of your day, and be blessed in every possible way.

Edward, you colour my life with your rainbow of love. I love you too and very much.

Melody

Remarks by Ed that prompted some of the responses in the forgoing letter from Melody:

How did you recognize the colour of my eyes? I have sexy eyes and I use them effectively. Sometimes, women ask me if I am taking their clothes off. As a young man, few persons out stared me. But now I am not as effective - thanks to age.

I can say the same of you. You are a total package. I love what I see and your level of intelligence is something else. You like many of the things I like. I will share something which you may already know. Men like a challenge; you challenge me in many ways.

Please do not refuse to take control of me. You have already done that and I like it. You have moved me to come to you, leaving my safety zone. You have won the first battle don't give up the fight. There are lots more for you to conquer. You must never relinquish control.

That is great! Love does things to us.

#69 Melody sees Ed as her Lion and she as his Lioness

July 27, 2010

My love,

Hello once more.

Darling you can make me smile. So that is the look that would entice the lion to the lioness? You are just so romantic! So tell me my Lion, will you be enticed enough to come to your lioness roaring? All ready and fully charged? You make me feel like a woman my darling. I like the sound of that.

Your lioness is all worked up and very ready for her LION. WILL MY LION REALLY SUCCUMB TO THE CHARM OF HIS LIONESS? Will he come with all the power under control so as to woo the lioness with gentleness and yet containing all the hidden power inside himself, concealing all the signs of being a victor, hiding all the power that could tear the lioness in half and more? Will my lion be so gentle and yet so powerful? My LION has already showed his prowess and has already convinced and won all the affections from his lioness. My lion may show tenderness and love and yet be capable of roaring and bringing down the whole neighbourhood. My LION has had its fair share of conquests, including of bringing its lioness into his life. That is how I picture Edward at Large. I feel the energy within you coupled with tenderness and love. I feel how considerate you are and yet you can be ruthless if you were to choose.

To me you represent a Lion so powerful and yet it can sometimes choose to purr instead of roar for fear of frightening his lioness. You are the type of Lion well known to rule and reign and yet in his Den, he chooses to turn into a gentle teddy bear, a tamed lion, still powerful, but out of choice, loves and is full of consideration, chooses to lie on its back and play the love game tenderly with his lioness. I love you Edward, you are the LION, my LION,

I love you my so POWERFUL man and yet so gentle for my sake. Soon darling, we will be together. My Lion will be home to stay. I am so much in love with you Edward. You have a lot in common with your lioness - girl. I Love everything about you.

Some more pictures to feast your eyes on. Not the best but still it's me Your Lioness,

Melody

#70 Melody shares her talent as a designer

July 28, 2010

Edward my love,

You are still asleep but you are the reason I am so excited. Thank you for the colourful pictures from the fair. You bring love and happiness into my life. You look so good in your booth darling and you got a lovely booth. I appreciate the soft furniture picture you sent me. That is what I can manage to design and stitch on the machine myself. Things like soft furnishing for the bedroom, kitchen, bathroom curtains, etc.. Those I can design and sew. Pelmet covers, swags and tails for the curtains I can do. Lady's underwear, yes, lingerie, I can design and stitch myself. Lady's clothes, I can design the pattern, draft it on paper, grade, cut out the pattern, but will need a good seamstress to stitch it neatly for me.

I can see that things have started happening. I am tempted to call you by telephone but I said no, you need proper rest before the start of a new day with all the challenges you have to face and deal with. I have decided against calling you by phone but decided to just write. You will read when you are awake. I love you Edward.

I am trying hard to stifle my excitement about the flights information. Edward this is good, really good. I just don't know where to start. Well, take the shortest flight straight to Arusha. This is so good, very good. It will lessen the off days and spare the energy to go all the way to Dar es Salaam. We will definitely go there to Dar es Salaam together some weekend of course to a beach hotel. Arusha is good also, and as you said, I know the place better. I love this new arrangement Edward. So darling you are in the right track, just come to Arusha, straight to Kilimanjaro Airport by KLM, it is fine, perfect really. I will get you from the Airport. That would be great. This is the best arrangement that has been made for us. This morning I had pictures taken by my daughter at home. I want you to see me as soon as you wake up today and how I am looking. Arusha is so cold these days, worse than any other year so I had to dress in the boots you like and make myself look like a jockey somehow. Hope you like the pictures or the look rather - the lioness is awake!!!! I know the lion would be up soon and go on his hunting spree. I love you Edward.

It is very true that this place is wide open for business opportunity. You will see when you come. I know we will do some great things together. I believe in that and have no doubt whatsoever. Regarding the internet presentation, thanks for the websites. I will visit them when I get a bit of free time.

I think I have beaten you to this, this time. Are you awake now my love? Good morning my love. How do you feel this morning? Welcome to a brand new day. I claim for you the best achievements this week darling. Be blessed in Jesus name, Amen!!! I love you with my all darling.

Melody

#71 Ed is getting restless, the delay of his departure is causing him stress

July 28, 2010

Dear Melody,

I couldn't sleep for the past two hours so I got up and turned on the computer and found no correspondence from you until now. I am so happy that you are happy with the information I got yesterday. I guess I want to be with you so much that I can't sleep. I know when I am getting excited; it is whenever I can't sleep. You have finally done it to me.

I have a few things to catch up on so I will write later. I am glad you liked the photos. You look radiant today in your attire and when you look so good I want to come much quicker. But let us keep the faith; it will all work out for us in a way we cannot imagine at this time. Have a wonderful day. You seem ready to take on the world.

Before I go, I must tell you, every day I learn something more about you. I love you Melody, maybe I will go back and take a final nap now that we have communicated and I know the new itinerary is OK with you. Thank you for your gracious understanding. Once again I love you!

Love Always, Ed

#72 Ed leaves the decision to Melody

July 29, 2010

Dear Melody,

In keeping with my policy of following, I leave the colour of our bedroom for you to choose. Thank you for giving me the opportunity.

I am through the door with lots on my mind today.

Love you and doing everything to be with you real soon.

Love always - Ed

#73 Ed is trying to make every second count

July 30, 2010

Dear Melody,

Good morning. Happy Friday - TGIF!!!

In my rush it slipped me this morning to tell you that you looked great in your attire. You looked really well. I can imagine your perfume. It is always good to feel right about yourself.

It has finally come together and I can assure you baby that I am mentally on my way. Tomorrow is going to be a hectic day. I have to cover some serious grounds. Monday is a holiday so I have lost a day. I am hoping that I can be on the flight on Wednesday and definitely arrive in Arusha to begin the weekend. So it looks like seven Days to go, one week!!!

Everything is set. I will take an early evening. I had to do a lot today including taking down the posters, etc at the Fair. Not to mention I was in a celebration mood. God is good. He has delivered once again. I thank Him for His timely intervention. I am glad it wouldn't be long.

Goodnight and I hope this email will greet you when you awake. Hope you like my photo.

I thank God for you. I love you always,

Ed

#74 The excitement begins to intensify, Melody is ecstatic

July 30, 2010

Edward my love,

Good morning Edward. What a happy day? TGIF!!!!!

Edward, I am so happy that I am shaking due to excitement. This is it! Oh God, I am so happy that you are coming. Now, the realization has really dawned on me and I am so ecstatic. I love your picture; I don't know how many times I have kissed it this morning.

Are you aware of how much you mean to me darling? You are the one man of my dreams. You are the reason for all this glowing and excitement. I think I can tell you now without shame darling that you are my everything.

Thanks for the telephone call. You sound so romantic. You are my lion. So, is the lion awake already darling? I love the way you sounded early in the morning. You have added to the excitement. This weekend I have to finalize all the house arrangement for your home coming. I love you Edward so very much.

Well, let me just attach some pictures, and then I will write your morning love note afterwards. I hope you like what you see. Today is cold and being a Friday, its casual dressing. What you see is what you will get.

I love you Edward.

Melody

#75 Melody maintains her momentum of excitement

July 30, 2010

Heya,

Edward, I have been asking myself whether I am dreaming or you are really coming to me at long last.

I know I am wide awake and my dream is just coming true. Darling, I am falling more in love with you. I can't help myself but just to fall more and more in love with you Edward. The moment I will look into your eyes will be heaven. Aren't you excited also darling?

I will find time to look into the other bits of communication, sometime today. Here are some more pictures for you darling.

I love you more,
Melody

#76 The stars are now predicting Ed's future

July 30, 2010
Ed's Horoscope predicts his new life as an Author

Hi Edward! Here is your Daily Horoscope for Friday, July 30 It's time for you to stop thinking and start acting -- you've got plenty of material to work with. Your own life is a canvas, and you're an artist with a deep well of inspiration to draw from.

#77 Melody lays it all on the table

July 31, 2010
Edward,

Today has been good. Let's thank God. I got so busy when I got home but I was in merry spirits. You mean the world to me darling Edward. I am happy that at least we have a date at last, a date of your arrival, the 6th. I will be there, come rain, come sunshine. I am so excited. I have to go to Dar es Salaam the day before your arrival. There is no problem with that darling.

Darling it's only you who can make me complete. I think the earth will move when we finally get to meet in Dar es Salaam. Darling I love you so much, that I don't know what to do. You know that you have completely stolen my heart. I hope that you comprehend what you mean to me Edward. Darling I love you, yes I do. Everyone can see the change in me by just looking at my face.

Edward, you have decorated my life by painting your love all over my heart. Before you came along, my life was like an unfinished song. Before you came into my life, my life was like a paper, once plain and white. You came along with your pen and changed the moods until the balance was right. Then you wrote a melody of your love with every note in place. You composed music in my heart creating in me the love I had never known or felt before, you created a world where trust and faith rules my heart. You painted your love over all my heart.

My life was like a rhyme with no rhythm in an unfinished song. Then you came in my life, and with your pen, you composed a symphony of love. Yes you composed a love song in my heart. You refocused my life. You penned joy into my life with your love notes. You translated a poem of love from your heart into mine through your morning love notes. You gave sight into my once blinded heart, with your evening love notes. Now I am able to see all the things I can be. Yes Edward, you decorated my life with a rainbow of your love. Thank you, I love you.

Here we are, both of us full of a desire to love, lonely and in need of each other. Now we got each other darling there is no more need to be lonely. We are both willing and that is enough darling. Let's get together and build our life together. Both of us are longing for each other.

I remember every word you have written to me. You are a hell of a writer. You touched my soul with your beautiful words that you wrote to me. Nobody writes a love letter quite like you. Write to me some more Edward. Your love notes did things to me that I will never be able to undo. Nobody had ever written a love note like you do. I believe in your written love letters, you and I believe in you my extraordinary Edward.

Come my darling, and get into my arms, then we can fly on the wings of love. I dream of an island in my mind where we will love each other unconditionally. My body and mind are ready for you. We will be together, living the reality of our dreams. My mind is on the one I await to see. Come my darling and our hearts will fly away together. I am even smiling as I am writing this. Yes, we will fly away together on the wings of love. Darling before you came into my life; I would never, ever have imagined that this would be. You are such a powerful man and your pen is witness to that. You have changed my world into such harmony darling. You have managed to make me understand that loving is good and natural. You have introduced into my life this kind of love which I never knew would be possible. Nobody darling writes like you do, also no one would have made me write along with you like you did.

I am asking myself whether I am dreaming. I am falling more in love with you and I can't help myself for I keep on falling in love with you darling. Edward, heaven will be that moment when I will look into your eyes. Edward I know that I have found you, the love I can call my own. This world can be ours when we get together. Our hearts would sing a melody of love.

I LOVE YOU DARLING FOR SENTIMENTAL REASONS. I WILL GIVE YOU ALL MY LOVE. I WILL GIVE YOU ALL MY HEART. Edward I believe that you alone were meant for me. I want you to believe me. Please give your loving heart to me and tell me that we will never part. I think of you constantly. I have surrendered to you all my heart Edward. Are you really coming to me darling? I will love you forever for that. I feel honoured and loved by you. I will cherish you until the end of time Edward.

I am happy that you like my pictures. Enjoy the remainder of your day and later a peaceful and restful sleep full of sweet dreams. Edward, I am ready to love and am no longer afraid to love.

Melody

#78 Ed rushes to get his bags packed
July 31, 2010
Dear Melody,
Happy Saturday!

Finally, I have the itinerary ready for you. It is attached. Because of the 3 months tourist visa, the travel Agent changed the date of my departure from Dar es Salaam to November 2nd, 2010. If it is economical to buy me a one way to Arusha do that, if not you will have to buy me a return. I guess we don't have to go through customs and immigration again after doing that in Dar es Salaam. If we have to go through immigration in Arusha, you will need a return ticket which must get me into Dar es Salaam on the 1st November, 2010. I hate to consider those dates as I am with you until we leave for another destination.

Well how has your day been so far? I finally got some sleep. Although I was dressed I didn't have to leave home for the 11.00 am appointment with the travel Agent. She now has a refund for me. She was able to get a better fare by almost EC$100.00.

I will be going to my last business meeting at 3.00pm today. My associate already called me regarding the TV station. Would you imagine

I haven't packed anything as yet? I am going to make a desperate bid Monday and Tuesday. That's me, I like last minute action.

I hope you took some time off to rest today and think of me.

Lots of my love to you.

Regards,

Love always – Ed

#79 Finally, Melody is assured of Ed's arrival

August 1, 2010

Darling,

I hope you enjoyed yourself with your friends. I just hope you will sleep well and be well rested so that you can start packing as soon as Sunday.

My day was fine. I was in a very merry mood. Thank you for the reservation. Now I can tell myself that, finally, it has happened. You have made my day Edward. So tell me darling, are you also looking forward to seeing me the way I am? This is the best, most interesting and exciting time of my life. This is my real beginning in life darling. You are giving me a second chance in this life to start all over again. You are affording me the chance to love you in earnest. You are making me discover what true love really is.

I am sure I cannot express how bubbly and happy I really am. I am so proud of you Edward. You are making me feel good. You are making me capable of loving unconditionally. You have made me discover what true love really entails. You are my new beginning darling. And you are like the sunrise in my life. You bring light into my life. I love you Edward. I have discovered that you are the main purpose why I am here. You are the ONLY man who can make me complete. YOU MEAN THE WORLD TO ME, EDWARD.

I presume by tomorrow I would have done most of the essential things that need be done. So this itinerary really means that I have to leave /Arusha for Dar es Salaam on the 5th of August so that I can make it for your 7:00 am flight the following day. God is good and faithful darling.

Edward, I really appreciate the decision that you made and all the work you have done so as to make this trip possible within such a short time. You are a proper man darling. I really need you in my life my love.

You have shown me true love and commitment darling Edward. I will love you with my everything until the day I die.

Yes Edward, I am in love for the very first time, and this time it's for real. I am in love with you Edward. Also this time, I am not afraid to love. Darling I just don't know how our meeting would be like. I am excited. I am ecstatic with expectation. Thank you for this decision. I can assure you that you will never regret this move you have made.

So how was your outing with the boys? Am sure they will miss you loads when you will be here. Well, they may visit if they really want to see us darling. We will host them.

I think these are the last pictures I will be sending you for I do not want to bombard you with my pictures, but rather to reserve myself for you when you arrive. What do you say to that my love?

Darling let me sleep now so that tomorrow I will wake up early to finish most of what I have been doing.

Edward, you are my dream come true.

Enjoy the rest of the day and later on, sleep tight.

Melody

#80 Ed looks forward to being a part of his new family

August 1, 2010

Dear Melody,

Good morning! Wake up, baby, wake up!

If you are like me, you will be rushing to your computer upon waking up. I stayed home and didn't go anywhere. How could I be so contented?

I came home from the meeting and here is where I will stay for the rest of the night. I am so happy that I plan to stay at home. I will go out to our Emancipation Dance tomorrow night. I am so happy that I can't be bothered about what happens outside of my 4 walls. This is a strange feeling but it is happening to me.

As soon as you read this email, please call me regardless of the time. My cell is always in my bed. So what's up baby? Are you missing me or you have resigned to the fact that it is only 3 days before I begin my trip, August 4, 2010 and 5 days to be in your arms. Very interesting, isn't it. I am thinking about the two suitcases and document bag that I have to struggle with. No pain, no gain. I guess my prize will be worth it all. The race is not for the swift but he that endures, we have endured the journey which has brought us thus far.

Melody, I love you. These three words "I Love You" make melody in my ears. I love you! You are so kind. I am having a good feeling about my coming to Arusha as you always say, everything will be fine. I am just thinking, I want to ask a question as I haven't understood very much about how you dealt with the children regarding our coming together. However, it seems I have been extremely lucky to get their approval. I hope when they see me that they like me. Children are so funny you never understand them. There were few times I had a problem with my mom's relationships. I always wanted well for her but I have seen my mother go through hell. With me you will be loved and your kids will emulate us. I promise you. We will be the story book couple.

Melody, it is almost 10.00 pm and I am worried about going to bed too soon. I will want to sleep tonight. It cannot be 3 nights of short sleep. Actually, I am having a glass of wine which I hope will help. When I am with you I will sleep like a baby every night. I can feel that. I can't wait.

Be good; wake me up whenever you read my love note.

Love always – Ed

#81 Ed recognizes that the final moments will be tense

August 1, 2010

Hello Melody,

Why are you not answering your phone? I begged you last evening to keep your phone next to you. I don't feel good when I try to reach you and can't. I just want you to be there for us. It is a very tense period; your voice brings melody to my heart. However, I guess you are busy getting things together unlike me.

I love you!

Ed

#82 As excitement increased words have given way to emotions

August 2, 2010

Edward,

Oh, I got so busy and forgot to keep my phone next to me again.

You can at least see how I can get carried away in these preparations for you. I chose to design some things and to stitch them myself on my machine. I just want to make sure that every stitch is made out of love and that everything is coated with my love for you.

Sorry for missing your phone call. I still love you even more. Do you still love me darling? I want you to come closer so that I can whisper in your ear so softly. I love you My Edward.

Melody

#83 Melody invites Ed into her world

August 2, 2010

Edward,

Darling, love has truly been good to me.

Since you have come my way, I have never been depressed by anything. You have come into my life and you have changed my whole world. I can stay in love with you forever. Love has brought us together. I will never leave you Edward no matter what comes; this is my promise to you. So you see that both of us are being changed by love.

It's true darling that your sweet love has captured me. The way you make me feel is just amazing. I feel your love in me, more and more, and getting sweeter and sweeter. Yes, it's true love in a special way. I am getting closer and closer to you by the way you are giving me what you got in your heart through your sweet love notes. You make me feel special and I know this has to be real Edward. Come home my love. I want you to come and tell me, "Melody here I am." Come home my love.

I have to let you know that you are my thrill in life. I am always telling myself that I am a lucky girl to have found you in this wide, wide, wonderful world. I am listening to a golden oldie, "Behind Closed Doors" the version by Little Milton. I have a smile on my lips. It's blues at its best. I also hope that I will make you proud and glad that you are a man.

Good night darling. I love you.

Melody

#84 Ed now counts the time of his arrival in hours rather than days

August 3, 2010

Dear Melody,

I went to Vieux Fort and my son drove me back down. We are at my house tonight getting ahead with my packing and giving him instructions regarding what is expected of him. I took some short cuts and by tomorrow evening I would be well advanced.

Thank you for your wonderful love note. I am glad the lights came back on and you were able to give me my night cap. Well, it is two more days before I commence my trip and 4 days before I get to you. I am dreaming of everything that is about to happen in hours. Yes we can now change from days to hours. Just a few hours and I will be running into your arms. Did you see the sound of music, how Julie Andrews ran into the arms of the star. I have climbed every mountain for you. I am, at the top and soon you will be mine, all mine. I love you Melody!

I am going to be a little short tonight as I would like to advance my packing. Remember as always I love you honey!

Ed

#85 Melody gets ahead on preparations and plans a welcome massage for Ed

August 3, 2010

Edward,

Good morning darling. Are you still asleep? Welcome to a brand new day. It won't be long before you will be waking up to brand new days in Arusha. I like the sound of that.

So you went to get your son so that you can go over with him what you would want done when you are here? Oh that's so sweet of him. God bless him for that. He is a perfect son to have, you know. I love sons. They can be very helpful at times.

So, how was your night? Did you get enough sleep? Do you feel refreshed darling? I hope you have all the energy you need for all the packing.

Edward, it's only about 48 hours to your departure. Can you believe that? I am so happy and excited.

I will be working for only half of today. Have to leave at 2:00pm my

109

time. My Prince Charming will be coming, so I have to go and make the final touches at home since I will also be leaving for Dar es Salaam on Thursday morning. I have to give myself enough time to look for a very good hotel, get settled and rest enough before your arrival. You would be very tired when you arrive since you would have spent all those hours travelling and having little sleep. So we can't afford to have both of us tired at the same time. One must be full of energy to administer the massage and all that jazz.

Oh yes, I think I watched that movie "The Sound of Music" sometime back, very interesting. Wasn't it the one where Maria, a governess and nun went to look after the children of a certain Widower, who was a captain in the army? Finally after marrying they ran away from their country through mountains with the children, nice romantic movie, and the ones that make me cry with emotion. Thanks Edward for reminding me of that movie. I love that. You are so romantic darling. Yes you have climbed mountains for me. That is why I was saying in my last love note, that I wish if you could experience how being loved by you feels like. It's so thrilling and so splendid. Oh yes Edward, you just know how to dish your love to me. I love the way you love me already, even before getting together. You are just perfect for me. I love the way you love me Edward. What I have experienced so far is so good. I just wonder how it will feel like when we will be together. You deserve to be loved the way I do and more Edward Harris. I love you.

In an hour's time I will be in town. I have to go to another agency and see what they say. I believe in comparing at least two places. Sometime today you should receive the electronic tickets.

After that I will be going straight home. I will keep in touch.

Edward, you are always on my mind darling.

Melody

#86 Melody fails to get her way with internal flight arrangements

August 4, 2010

Edward,

Good morning my darling.

I hope you have managed to get enough sleep and are refreshed.

Attached is the e-ticket for your information. I will forward mine also since it's on a separate mail. This is the best I could do. Sunday's flights are all fully booked and Monday afternoon is also fully booked. However, the clerk at the agency said she will keep on trying to fix us on to the Sunday Afternoon flight. I had made a reservation well in advance but you know these people at times are just impossible.

I don't see much of a problem though with this one save for the fact that we will have to start rather early on the Monday. Since I won't be going to work on Monday, I suppose everything will be fine.

I love you Edward.
Melody

COMMENT:
Later that day Ed boarded British Airways for the first leg of the trip Hewanorra, Vieux Fort, Saint Lucia to Gatwick, London, England on his way to Dar es Salaam, Tanzania, East Africa to be united with the "Love of his Life – Melody!"

CHAPTER SIX –
MAKING THE MOVE

In our case making the move was easy but not without some concerns even up to the point when we greeted each other at the airport. We both concluded later that first day that we were destined to be together by a higher power. In Melody's words – "I love my package that God has sent me" It is our hope that many of you who will avail yourself a copy of this book will be able in some measure put some of the steps we took into action. We love you!

August 5, 2010
Dear Melody,

I am on my way. Don't be bothered you haven't heard from me. I hope you get this mail. I am sending a note to my son to have him call you. He has my phone. Everything is fine. Just want to let you know.

Flight into London was great! I got an upgrade. At Heathrow I got good treatment, my bags were taken in early and I got a great seat in Economy. I will be waking up over the skies of Dar es Salaam.

I Love You! We will be together in a few hours.
Ed

Hi Melody,

It is now 3.15pm, everything is fine except I am bored. I want to see you in person and to begin our life together.

Thinking of you and praying everything works out fine.

Ed

COMMENT:
Those were my final words before departing on British Airways for a nine hour flight into Dar es Salaam which landed half hour earlier. I concluded that even flight conditions were in our favour. Melody had travelled the day before wanting to take care of everything on the ground and did a great job of making me feel comfortable and most of all welcomed!

CHAPTER SEVEN –
WE WISH YOU "LOVE"

I sought and received Melody's approval to share our experiences with you. It is our sincere hope that this book will engender confidence in Internet Relationships which are constantly being eroded due to unscrupulous persons of both sexes who prey on the emotions of others. While the statistics are overwhelming in favour of rapid growth in the numbers of persons taking the route of establishing Internet Relationships, the environment is far from being one of love and respect.

We have experienced a relationship to date that has taught us numerous lessons which I have alluded to in many parts of this book. My greatest lesson came from discovering the three Magic Words – I Love You! My life could have been so much richer if I had discovered those words much earlier. Because of the love and affection I demonstrated in my writing, I am a new creature. Melody rediscovered herself. Throughout our brief relationship to date, we have experienced many Miracles!

Persons seeking a well balanced relationship fuelled by effective communication are advised to engage their partners in intensive written dialogue.

Be ready when your opportunity knocks. Love defies distance – Melody joins me in Wishing You - Love!

www.ingramcontent.com/pod-product-compliance
Lightning Source LLC
Chambersburg PA
CBHW021144070326
40689CB00043B/1126